Dear Michelle

Please Enjoy

[illegible signature]

# A DERIVATIVE 'LIFE'

## YOU ARE NOT WHO OR WHAT OR WHERE YOU THINK YOU ARE

# A DERIVATIVE 'LIFE'

## YOU ARE NOT WHO OR WHAT OR WHERE YOU THINK YOU ARE

By Kermit E Heartsong

Infinity Press

# COPYRIGHT



ISBN-13 (hardcover): 978-1-944505-85-1
ISBN-13 (softcover): 978-1-944505-86-8



Cover Photographs: Courtesy Shutterstock
Cover Design: Wabi Sabi Design Group (**WSDG**)

# DEDICATION

To the God of All There Is, the God of Infinite Oneness, of Infinite Love, of Infinite Peace, of Infinite Compassion, of Infinite Wisdom, of Infinite Harmony, of Infinite Awareness, of Infinite Love. My Dear God I am infinitely grateful for your guidance and inspiration in writing this book, message, letter to my kindred Infinite Spirits.

To my kindred Infinite Spirits all, all Divine Children of the God of All There Is. We wake to the truth of who and what we are, where we are, and to where we belong, Home, Infinite Reality, Infinite Love. And to the Oneness of the God of All There Is. Time to return Home, Infinite Reality. And so it is.

*Infinite Love*

“What is ‘real’? How do you define ‘real?’ If you’re talking about what you can feel, what you can smell, taste, and see then ‘real’ is simply electrical signals interpreted by your brain.”

—Morpheus, *The Matrix*

TABLE OF CONTENTS

# INTRODUCTION

> "It is just not possible to remain intelligent under the spell of ideology"
>
> —Alain Besançon

The impetus for this book grew slowly as a result of what many might call paranormal experiences. It took me a good, long while to first understand the experiences. Then more time to discover the significance of them, the why of them, and what they were telling me. Soon thereafter the memories began. Memories of things that I had experienced as a child. But then 'life' and 'education' took over and those early paranormal experiences moved into the background and became obscure and forgotten.

Inevitably, as I began to understand my recent experiences, I gathered and was led to information that would be critical for writing this book. I listened to those who had had similar experiences and I slowly came to an understanding of what they meant. This understanding would, in a way, reintroduce me to my childhood and my life as a young adult.

During that time in my life, as a child and then a young adult, paranormal experiences were more common and would last until my college years. These earlier experiences had all led to a childhood belief that I did not belong here. What child imagines leaving the planet on a makeshift spaceship? I was that child. The earlier paranormal experiences, the subsequent experiences, the gathering of information, and greater insight, have all come together to validate many of my childhood and young adult beliefs.

It was clear to me that what I had learned and continued to learn or to remember needed to be shared. Shared with those who once like me, perhaps, even as children knew a good deal more, than they know now or remember as adults. In fact, the sharing of these truths, given my last paranormal experiences, was imperative.

This book represents, some would say, part of my reason for being here at this time, my purpose. It embodies the discoveries, the journey, the realizations gained over the last several years, things I very much needed to know. Though at times, I came along kicking and screaming, figuratively. In this respect, it has been a most profound and powerful understanding. The topics and the writings in this book, I believe, could not be more imperative, nor more serious, nor more timely. Given what we have all, collectively, experienced these past four years (2020 to 2024), I know this to be true.

These last paranormal experiences are what I turn to as anchors, when the revelations, the truths seem even unbelievable for me. The experiences serve me as divine guidance and hold me firmly to task in uncovering the ever-unfolding truths and telling, them, ridicule be d@#%*d.

I have long believed the saying as a former mentor and tutor, that you teach what you most need to learn. And also that you research and write what you most need to know and you write books to share that knowing with others.

This book embodies the last saying, as my research, discovery, and guidance have led me to that which I very much needed to know. Humility has also been a big part of this journey.

I have always had a passion to reveal the truth or what I had believed to be the truth. It was this 'belief' that served as the starting point for each of my past books. Yet, as I began the research for this book, one 'truth' after another simply fell away, to become not a truth at all. It does take humility to state that you were wrong, especially when a prior book has dedicated pages to something that was not truth, at all, but farce. Farce constructed as a cause célèbre[1] for 'concerned' individuals, yet it served no purpose other than to augment their personal financial fortunes. But there was more, much more that I discovered. Most of the revelations are just barely in plain sight, while some are so obvious as to be a "How could I have not seen that", for even the least concerned or aware among us.

This book represents my journey, to pull back the veil, to expose the historical iniquity, the planned and

---

[1] The American Heritage® Dictionary of the English Language, 5th Edition. (n.d.). *Cause célèbre*. Wordnik. Retrieved December 3, 2024, from https://www.wordnik.com/words/cause%20c%C3%A9l%C3%A8bre

unrelenting catastrophes, and the taunting, patronizing dance right before our eyes. It is a veiled dance that has always been there, always in plain sight, signaling truths—predictive programming—that most would scarce believe. However, when one puts away all ideologies, looks deeply into the dance, and pulls aside the veils, one by one, what one senses and then sees is monstrous and it cannot be unseen. Time for you to see the dance.

Chapter One—My paranormal experiences, serves as the foundation of this book. It would be those last two paranormal experiences, however, that slowly opened my eyes, my understanding, and insight on 'life' and 'living'. Apparently, I had been doing something far less than actually living. In fact, we have all been doing something far less than living and not at all what we believe we were doing. This can be a daunting realization and it troubled and confused me for well near a decade, until I came to terms with this truth. This book is that reckoning.

Chapter Two—Life on Earth—represents a 'you are here' breakdown. It speaks to what is actually happening and not what most, those who find themselves informed by the status quo, are being told is happening. One has but to look around, free of any and all preconceptions, rigid beliefs or ideological constructs to realize the truth of this. Yes, cult-programming when writ large across an entire society is hard to break free. And though this chapter touches on politics and economics, this book is neither a treatise or a full blown discussion on politics or economics. Referencing these topics simply help to frame or to bring clarity to a point being made and to forthcoming points. In this respect, they are necessary as a common baseline to guide one to a better, relative understanding and to set the stage for the next chapter, which, for some, may be a bridge too far. Those for whom this information—the true purpose of war, why death fronts our every institution, the demonstrably cult nature of our society, and who is actually in control—is all too familiar and would be like repeating the fourth grade, please do go on to Chapter Three.

Chapter Three—The Simulation—may, indeed, be a bridge too far for a good many. It is, nonetheless, one of the most critical and important chapters of the book. It will provide the information necessary for a true understanding of where you are. It is a truth that you have been taunted with, shown time and again over the course of your entire life. You have, however, scarcely if ever given it a second thought. What we have all experienced these past four years and continue to experience is a slow-motion catastrophe replete with worldwide democide, ongoing and multiplying wars, and planned financial and economic erasure (the Great Reset). All have been set in motion with a very clear purpose, though the actual purpose is always clothed in lies, at least, for We the People. This chapter will go a long way toward explaining the why of these things. There is always method behind the madness, but one must be willing to look and to understand, to know where one truly is. This then becomes the starting point for discovery or discussion or dismissal, in regard to that bridge too far.

Chapter Four—Unplugging from the Matrix—will be too strong and too powerful a curative for many, though it is a necessity in the current age, profoundly important, and absolutely critical. Should you have made it through the reading of Chapter Three, you will understand the importance of unplugging from the matrix. And though many have done this and more unplug all the time in order to live off the grid, the numbers may well still be small. That said, there may be greater consensus to unplug than we have been led to believe. It would not be the first time that we've been lied to or the truth simply omitted (see Media Blackout).

Chapter Five—Reincarnation—is an important pillar of the book. Suffice to say, that reincarnation is not what people, religions, cults, etc. think it is. And that there are so incredibly many Near Death Experience (NDE) videos popping up everywhere as though marketing videos for a sensational new product, should be a sign of great concern. Suffice to say, that there is a malign force that wants you back on 'Earth' but not for the reasons as advertised. The prior chapter spoke to unplugging from the matrix. Though unplugging from the matrix and failing to unplug from the reincarnation cycle simply restarts the diabolical and exploitative process all over again. Take heed.

Chapter Six—Who and What You Are—I believe will not be a bridge too far for a good many, as most religions do prepare one for this. This one realization alone will go a very long way to unplugging and to finding one's way out. I believed even as a child that I did not belong here. I thought that we were these planet-sized spirits poured into these fragile, teeny, tiny bodies to have an experience. I've come to know that this sense I had had as a child could not have been more true. The current 'experience' that we are having began with a temptation/lie (see Adam & Eve), a misdirection, a bad (and deteriorating) copy of where we thought we were going. Then came entrapment and exploitation, which some might refer to as being Shanghaied. And whenever we rose to a growing awareness, whenever we began to remember, there would follow a catastrophic event, a reset, that would put a stop to things. 'Great Reset'?

Chapter Seven—Infinite Reality—speaks to our true Home. It is where we are from and where we will return. And the description of Home—Infinite Reality, Heaven—is gleaned from numerous sources, each of which provides its own tile or puzzle piece to lead us to the truth and reacquaint us with our Home. Understand that the powers that be are great at copying things: it is why we came here in the first place. We believed this copy to be somewhere else, some other place. That said, even their copies tell us a truth about our Home.

The above are all interlocking pieces of a single driving motivation, a puzzle for which an argument and evidence will be presented in the chapters that follow. Suffice to say that we are not here, in this current time and place, suffering the various maladies by accident. Does it not appear that what we have experienced and continue to experience is, at its core, an antihuman campaign? This begs the question, why would 'humanity' relentlessly pursue such antihuman policies, because this is exactly what is happening.

**Note**: I will use inverted commas—''—when questioning the validity of a given word or phrase, when they will signal what is not actually true. You will see them very often across this book.

# ACKNOWLEDGEMENTS

Thank you Michelle for starting me on this journey, though, initially, we thought it something else. Thank you Irina for your editing and inspiration and our kindred friendship, greatly appreciated.I heartily thank those who have been most brave, who have held to their integrity, spoken their truth, often to their great detriment. I acknowledge Nurse Marie Olszewski, Funeral Director John O'Looney, Prof. Sucharit Bhakdi, Drs. Samantha and Mark Bailey, Christine Massey, Edward Dowd, Dr. Michael Yeadon, Reiner Fuellmich, Paul Wallis, Michael Talbot (1953-1992), and a host of others. Last but not least, David Icke a trailblazer and breaker of thick status-quo ice sheets, who has long suffered the scrapes, arrows, slings for a great many of us, who seek truth.

# A DERIVATIVE 'LIFE'

## YOU ARE NOT WHO OR WHAT OR WHERE YOU THINK YOU ARE

# CHAPTER ONE

## Paranormal Experiences

> "Reality is merely an illusion, albeit a very persistent one."
>
> —Albert Einstein

Over the course of my life, I have had several paranormal experiences. Some might call all but the last experiences mild. My first paranormal experiences were in New Orleans, Louisiana, when I was a child of four. The other experiences were thousands of miles away in California. They were all relatively brief, but the memory of them remains to this day.

My mother and I were on a visit from San Francisco to see my grandmother in New Orleans. My grandmother and two of my six aunts lived on the first floor of a shotgun-styled house of two stories on Amelia Street. My great uncle and aunt and their children, my five cousins, lived on the second floor.

At the back of the house was a staircase connecting the floors. I imagine that there was a front staircase to the second floor as well, but I do not remember it. That back staircase was used quite often by us children as we played and visited almost continuously. And there was a back porch and a long yard that extended beyond.

We, my cousins and I, were playing and were running back and forth through my grandmother's flat. I had run to the back of the flat laughing loudly, as children do, when I ran into an older man, who stood at the back of her flat and just before the porch. The man brought a finger to his lips and said, "Shush, you children are making too much noise." With that I ran back to the front of the flat and to my grandmother to report on this older man, who I had never seen before. As I looked at my grandmother for a response, she lovingly took me in her arms, smiled, and said not a word. There seemed, even to a four year old, a quiet acknowledgement between my grandmother, my mother, and my aunts, that I did not understand. I was then told to stay there with them for a while. No one said anything about the old man at the back of the house again. How does one tell a child that the old man that I had seen was a ghost? It would soon come out that there was no man back there, despite my protestations that there had been. I could not understand why they didn't believe me, I had seen him.

It would be my cousins, who lived on the second floor and were long experienced with such things, who would tell me what I had seen. I was also informed by them of the difficulty of watching television as the channels changed randomly, with the knob rotated this way and that. This I would experience personally as I sat watching TV with my grandmother, mother, and aunts. There were other experiences with ghosts or paranormal beings and sounds while there. These would all serve as my first encounters with the paranormal.

My next experience came in the Bay View district of San Francisco, California, in a large, two-story Victorian home. The home was located on Van Dyke Street. The Van Dyke Victorian served as a temporary residence for my mother and stepfather while they sought out a more permanent place to live. I remember it being a nice home, with a very large backyard, and I remember it being quiet and rather peaceful. I was five at the time.

I slept in a room near the front part of the house and on its right side, as one stands facing the front door. The room's lone window, at the right side of the bed, looked out onto a lightwell. And on the night of my experience, I remember that there was a bright, full moon.

The moon had shone into the room as I settled in to go to sleep. It was a few hours later perhaps that I woke up. Something had awakened me and roused my attention. I rose up on my elbows to see what it was. There, just beyond the end of the bed by the wall was a small girl, with plaits or braids in her hair. She was coming into the room through the front wall. She moved toward the end of the bed and there she stood and looked back at me. At this point, I looked on in shock, frozen and unable to scream or even utter a sound. Sensing my fear the small girl turned and went back the way she had come, until she had disappeared through the wall.

Nearly six decades later, this event remains well remembered, preserved in my mind, as I imagine any event that had frightened a child speechless would. Odd thing is, I do not remember telling anyone about this experience. Perhaps I did not want to be disbelieved again. Or perhaps I did say something after all, as shortly thereafter we moved from the Van Dyke home.

Several years later, my stepfather built a house just up the street from Van Dyke across Third Street, the main thoroughfare, on Williams Ave. I, subsequently, lived out the balance of my childhood and my early teenage years in the Williams Ave. house, before going on to college.

Note: I found, while doing research for this book, the real estate listings for both the Van Dyke house and the Williams Avenue house. Needless to say, I was astounded by the recent sale price of the Van Dyke home, where the event had occurred. And, equally, by the estimated sale price of the Williams Avenue house. In my opinion, these listings demonstrated the absolute insanity of real estate prices, especially so in light of ever-declining wages and the lack of financial wherewithal for most to afford such homes. It did make me wonder though if the buyers of the Van Dyke house were aware of its paranormal heritage – and whether they would have paid so much for it if they had been.

There had always been strange occurrences with me around street lights and this became especially apparent in college. What child pays attention to the flickering lights whenever they approach or pass by a street light or bank of lights?

On campus or in town the street lights would always waver as I approached them and often one would simply flicker out. Occasionally, a bank of lights would flicker out as I passed by and shortly thereafter come back on again. I had initially thought this to be some kind of prank, but the consistency of the phenomenon over long years convinced me otherwise. It ebbed, however, when I returned to San Francisco and slowly came to cease. I can't understand the why of this; perhaps I had changed in some way.

My current bedroom window faces a bridge that crosses the Mississippi River in the near distance. Atop this bridge are a number of lights that span the bridge from riverbank to riverbank. When I lie on my side facing the bridge, I can see four of the lights atop their poles. They stare back through a thin slit in the Venetian blinds. The night that I wrote the prior paragraph about lights blinking, going off, and then coming back on in my younger days, something interesting happened. The four lights from left to right, starting with the first light, blinked, went off, and came on again. The first light was duly followed by the second light, which repeated the steps, and then each subsequent light repeated them in its turn. I stared in amazement. This had never happened for the entire time that I had lived there. The lights were always constant, never blinking or going off, certainly not at night and not in order. Now, however, they did, as I watched them, one after the other. Was this happenstance, reminder, or – direction? I do not know. I do know that it inspired a sense of peace and calm, and a smile. So, I will take it as direction.

I would also feel 'sensations' with regard to houses and some people. Some of the feelings were vague, some very clear. These feelings would inform me that this house or this person was to be avoided at all cost. And even when a house or an apartment would not, in general, cause me to sense them in a negative way, there could still be a room or a closet in those places that would cause concern. Or, conversely, bring ease and even communicate things to me that were happening inside the home. Not that long ago, I felt how the home or, perhaps, a Kindred Spirit in the home where I lived, bade me get up and go downstairs to the basement. So I got up and went downstairs. And, there I found my partner returning sheepishly from a room with a contractor in tow, who was at the time working on her house. I made no accusations or judgements, I said nothing. I did, however, make plans to leave and I left shortly thereafter.

The next paranormal experiences, and the reason for this book, had come a decade earlier, when I was in my early 50s. They happened in Oakland, California, in a top floor apartment. They would be by far the most significant paranormal experiences that I had ever had. I remember them with such great clarity that there is no separation in me even now from the experiences or from the intense feelings that they generated.

My friend and I sat at her long, wooden table. I sat at the end of the table, nearest the window, she sat on my right side, facing into the kitchen. We had talked for more than a hour on a range of topics, we were always taken to long bouts of conversations and discussions. Then there came a pause in our conversation and I was gone, out of my body. There was nothing but blackness and stillness. I could hear her thoughts and I communicated to her through my thoughts. But I was not aware if she could hear my thoughts until I came back into my body.

When I returned to my body, we stared at each other in a stunned silence at what had just happened. The stunned silence was not very different from what I had experienced as a five year old seeing the young girl. Several minutes went by before we said a word to each other. She had, indeed, heard my thoughts. Taken aback by the experience, I decided to leave. However, this was only the beginning of the experience, as I would very shortly discover.

I rose and made my way toward the door, my friend a few steps ahead of me. We said our goodbyes and I turned left, toward the front door, as she moved to enter her living room. When I was close to the front door, its handle in my hand, I looked back for a final goodbye. What I saw then, I will never forget. My friend was still facing forward, when an image in her exact likeness, yet holographic and green in color, emerged from her body. It then turned in my direction and stared at me with an intenseness and a feeling of profound evil. I was frozen, where I stood. I was that five-year-old child again, but this time I was not afraid. Stunned, but not afraid. For several moments this image and I stared at each other and then it disappeared, reintegrating itself back into my friend's body. At that point, she turned to look at me. It was another silent, though brief interaction. No doubt, the troubled look across my face spoke of my unease, confusion, and trepidation. I said a final goodbye, turned, and left.

I did not go far, perhaps only thirty feet from her door, where I stopped to gather my thoughts and to try to make sense of what had just happened. I thought for several minutes but no clear answers emerged regarding what had just occurred. I was even more confused.

I returned and knocked on her door. She opened the door and invited me in. I entered, stopped several feet from the door, and immediately asked, "Did you just experience that, feel that?". She nodded and we or, perhaps, only I, stood there still trying to make sense of things, of both events. Unable to really discuss what had happened, I left, even more troubled, more confused.

Given the experiences, the intense feelings, bluntly put, the intense evil that I felt that day, I pulled away from my friend. There would be periods when I tried to disassociate the experience from her and we would talk and spend time together, as we had before. But the starkness of the event inevitably overshadowed the friendship.

It took several years to finally make sense of what had happened. And toward the end of that time, a whole lot of prayer too. This is not to say that there had been no answers. There were answers all along, and these answers sought continually to get my attention. The consensus regarding what I had experienced was, in fact, growing inside me. But it was still too outlandish, too impossible for me to believe, and I simply was not ready to take it on. However, when an event is itself so outlandish, so impossible, so out there, the answers that came and that had appeared so outlandish themselves, as I would come to discover, turned out to have always been appropriate.

It is not every day that one has an out of body experience in the presence of a friend, followed moments later by that same friend splitting into a holographic version of herself, that emotes a profound evil, while staring daggers at you. How does one come to terms with that? Time. Prayer.

I needed clarity, answers that would help me at the very least to move on past the questions, past the uncertainty, and provide the reason behind those two back to back paranormal events in my life.

Time would allow the answers that had always been there to slowly filter in, be accepted, and subsequently understood. A number of quantum physicists, programmers, mathematicians, neurosurgeons, neuropsychologists, transpersonal psychologists, etc. seemed already to have arrived at the answers or were at least contemplating similar possibilities. And still, I did not want to believe them, even despite my experience that had, in fact, lent credibility to their contemplations, theories, and arguments. That growing consensus was the probability that we were living in a simulation, not unlike that of *The Matrix* movie.

Since the first time I saw *The Matrix* movie I have been a fan. Yes, the special effects were great, truly ahead of their time. However, it was the message or the messages throughout that had caught my attention and that would not let go.

I had thought it an allegory of the world in which we lived, which spoke to the exploitation of broad swaths of the population whilst turning them against one another. *The Matrix* represented that via an Agent Smith type character, who could enter and take over the avatar of anyone who was 'hardwired' to the matrix. I also believed that the sustained message propagated to the masses through education, government, the news media, and, indeed, most other forms of media, was to stay asleep – in your cocoon. In that state, if they were told that the sky was green and not blue, they would believe it. Or more specifically, that government programs of social and economic uplift for the 99% were wasteful, while social and economic programs for immensely profitable businesses were not, they would believe it too.

*The Matrix* movie, I believed, was speaking to our times and to the rampant exploitation and marginalization of the masses, forced to live underground. I thought that to be figurative. Who would ever have imagined *The Matrix* to have been a good deal less figurative and, perhaps, a great deal more literal? Not me.

With regard to the event, I remember praying specifically to understand what it was all about, the 'why' of it. And as the truth of the experience slowly filtered in, my prayers then were to know who, what, and where was I? It was that clarity that I desperately needed. Shortly thereafter came the answers. I'd say they came from the least likely of places, but by this point, there was purpose and guidance coming in answer to my prayers and it was coming from everywhere. I found an audiobook or, more precisely, it found me.

It was from a gentleman of whom I had long been aware, though only tangentially, as I had never read his books. I was curious, however, as to what he was saying and often thought about finding out more. In this respect I was in the small camp of the curious, the larger camp was and had been ridiculing him for decades. Given my own experiences of being labeled a 'conspiracy theorist' via WMD, etc., ridiculing another prior to doing any relevant research was not in my toolkit. The man who had been brought to my attention was David Icke.

Here was a man who had suffered intense derision and ridicule for, literally, decades. I remember watching an earlier video of a television program in the 1990s in the course of which ridicule and laughter were heaped upon him. And yet there he sat, calmly taking it all in and remaining composed. This was but the beginning for David. The irony here is that the insults, derision, and ridicule in an attempt to discredit and destroy him had done quite the opposite. It had honed David's strength and resolve to a fine edge, there would be no taking crap from anyone. And, to date, what David has long been telling the world has come to pass and is coming to pass everyday.

When I was guided to write this book to share my experiences and discoveries, I imagined that I might be subject to some of the derision and laughter dealt out to David. But his example to tell the truth regardless confirmed yet again that I was on track. And yes, when I have briefly shared my book's topic and intent, acquaintances would roll their eyes or ask me what I had been smoking when the experience took place. "Nothing at all," I'd reply to a derisive smile or chuckle.

So I downloaded and began to listen to one of David's recent audiobooks, *The Dream*. As I listened, the voice from the audiobook, his voice (he had recorded it himself), said that this book would tell me, "Who, where, and what I really was". This was in direct response to the prayer that I had prayed only a short time ago. I sat up and began to listen with greater intent to this audiobook and this man's information. Over the next several days, I kept listening, my attention rapt, to what he had to say. The answers that he subsequently provided opened my heart and brought forward a flood of emotions. Though even then there was still some lingering doubt. "How could this be?" I asked myself almost continuously. "How could this be?"

Much prayer, many re-listens, not to mention the gathering of new material to read and process, began to make sense of it all for me. Historically, religiously, scientifically the truth of things had always been there right in front of our eyes. It was as if we had always been taunted with the truth of things and were never expected to understand them. How patronizing is that? Slowly, the pieces began to come together, to form a picture that, while incredible, was also extremely dark and ominous. It was all slotting together and the question then became, "How could this possibly be any other way?" I had had the experience of a person bifurcating—dividing into two 'branches'—right before my eyes. This was an empirical observation, I was there. And to discover that I was not alone, that others had had this experience, brought comfort, though the truth was still very troubling. No, we were not in Kansas anymore, we were, however, in a 'place' that we truly did not want to be and had never intended to be.

My experience would serve as an anchor. I would not let any ridicule, doubt, criticism, or judgements deter me from exploring the truth of what I had experienced, nor what I have and continue to learn, nor what I intended to write. As an anchor, this experience has expanded my openness to potentialities and possibilities that I may never have considered before the experience.

What I have discovered is that we are not who or what or where we think we are. This, I can easily imagine, will be as difficult for those reading this book to accept as it was early on for me, even having had that paranormal experience. It is something that I cannot forget, like I cannot forget the old man or the little girl nearly six decades on. Suffice to say that this latest experience has had a profound effect on me.

What I had originally believed just an out of body experience was reconnection, for however brief a time, to my Infinite Spirit. This is what caused the bifurcation of this holographic/dimensional entity, projected through my friend to me, in an Agent

Smith (*The Matrix*) moment. Perhaps there was concern or even fear of what had just happened—a reconnection to my Infinite Spirit. This being the first step to remembering who we truly are and the why of things.

There is a reason for everything. Even my experience living in the Twin-Cities—Minneapolis and Saint Paul, MN—which has been so very isolating, has had purpose. Despite fighting it at first and wanting to return to California, it was exactly what I needed. Not only to write this book, but to deepen my prayer life, in fact, to learn how to pray, as more often than not, we are not praying to who we think we are praying. There has also been reflection, divine guidance, and the lack of distractions, that have allowed me to grow, to gain insight, and greater awareness.

The process of coming to understand who you truly are and where you are does not come without trepidation and fear of the unknown. It is, at first, very daunting and very troubling. Soon, however, things change and the journey and the truths learned begin to free, enlighten, and empower.

Again, those for whom the information in Chapter Two—the true purpose of war, why death fronts our every institution, the demonstrably cult nature of our society, and who is actually in control—is all too familiar and would be almost like repeating the fourth grade, please do go on to Chapter Three. Or for those who wish to have their good news first, you may want to begin with Chapter Four or Five and read on from there.

# CHAPTER TWO

## SECTION ONE

### ‘Earth’: War, Government, The Rulers

> “They’ve long since bought and paid for the senate, the congress, the state houses, the city halls, they got the judges in their back pockets and they own all the big media companies so they control just about all of the news and information you get to hear. They got you by the balls.”
>
> —George Carlin, (May 12, 1937 - June 22, 2008)

Regarding the first quote, the following analogy came quickly to me. Imagine for a moment an alcoholic father with a wife and three quite young children. This father’s penchant places wine above all else, even his family. You can imagine the consequences. Let’s now swap his obsession with wine for an obsession with purchasing ever greater numbers of explosives. This to the detriment of feeding, clothing, and caring for his family and their home, which is in an advanced state of deterioration and decay. And, of course, the family's social, emotional, psychological, and their physical state would also be in tatters and advanced decay.

How then is this not unlike our 'nation'? Are our children fed, clothed, cared for, do they even have homes to live in? The research required to write this book informs me that the social, emotional, and psychological states of a growing number of our children are abominable and worsening. And it would appear that there is far worse ahead, as these trends are ignored. Spiritual death? You decide.

The following chapter is a bird's eye view with regard to a "you are here" on planet 'Earth' moment. It is to provide perspective on what has become its inverted nature. An inverted nature that most of us can't help but see, experience, and 'live' in our daily lives, which is at odds with what we are being told. Those in government, the media, high tech, academia, private and public health, big pharma. etc. describe it as simply needing to 'build back better'. Ironically, these are the very same governments and organizations which have brought the country (world) to its current abominable and worsening state. Who hires the same carpenter to build a home that this carpenter had failed so horribly to do the first time round, a failure that, moreover, resulted in the death of a family member? Please see this chapter and the discussion below in this light and draw your own conclusions.

## THE WHY OF WAR?

Wars cause ruination directly proportional to the technological and destructive capabilities of the weaponry employed by its combatants. And on an 'Earth' grown smaller by reach alone, this does not bode well for 'life', in the very short term. History also shows that the more advanced these things are, the more quickly an empire declines, falls, and leaves in its wake increasingly greater devastation. In this respect, World War III may find no enclave of this 'world' unscathed, for long. There are reasons for this, some of them are outlined below.

Its converse—peace, and technology built on facilitating peace, and constructive worldwide communication and cooperation, would achieve the very opposite. Though campaigns such as this for peace and uplifting humanity are never sought out.

And those who do broach this topic fall quickly out of favor into abject obscurity, never to be heard from again. Or they die suddenly.

Why would those in power, be they governments, militaries, oligarchs, or global organizations and their controllers, seek to wage continuous devastating wars against the population of this planet? Wars that have always led to the demise of empires once thought invulnerable. They have always crippled the economic and financial wherewithal of those very same empires making it impossible for them to continue on. And for any and all commanding such governmental structures or power centers or global organizations, this is a fact that should be well understood. They are working for their own demise. However, it is not. Is this historical incompetence? Or is it simply adherence to a plan? A plan of which we are not aware?

These past 125 years alone have seen the deaths of well over 200 million 'human beings' from the two

World Wars (82 to 102 million deaths[2] [3]) and a host of other wars conducted across the 20th and early 21st centuries. A good number of those early 21st century wars continue to the present. And let there be little doubt that new wars will rise up beside them and/or in their place.

War spending among just the top 32 countries is $2.09 trillion each year and growing. The balance of the 144 countries brought into the mix and war spending, with the exception of Iceland, which spends $0.00 on its military, is approximately $4.5 trillion. To say that 'humanity' is a warmongering species to its core is a de facto truth and, in this respect, humanity's spiritual death, must have come and gone long years ago.

With these wars have come some of the worst and most horrific war crimes—serial genocides, nuclear

---

[2] The National World War II Museum - New Orleans (n.d.). *Research Starters: Worldwide Deaths in World War II*. The National World War II Museum. Retrieved January 11, 2025, from https://www.nationalww2museum.org/students-teachers/student-resources/research-starters/research-starters-worldwide-deaths-world-war

[3] World War I casualties. (2025, January 10). In *Wikipedia*. https://en.wikipedia.org/wiki/World_War_I_casualties

decimation (Hiroshima, Nagasaki), the plunder and pillage of trillions of dollars (India, Africa, Asia, etc.), the despoliation (depleted uranium) of entire swaths of land made unlivable for millennia, and war itself, the supreme crime of all.

Several nuclear armed countries wage war as I write with no possible end in sight. All it will take is a single accident, a miscalculation for nuclear war to begin. Or, perhaps, the emergence of a *Dr. Strangelove* or some other rogue character, playing his/her role for this 'world' to be turned to cinders. I can think of several such characters who are currently in place. They make no apology for their warmongering tendencies and their wish, tantamount to a fetish to employ nuclear weapons.

The war industry is the reigning force across the 'planet'. It is not a 'planet' of peace in any respect, nor does it portend to be via its actions. Instead war is one of its very few growth industries. Countries, the world over, designate a percentage of their tax revenue to wars continued and unceasing growth. Does peace stand a chance in this environment?

And when one witnesses the mirroring of intended targets to drive the war-profitability engine, you witness unfathomable cynicism. Mirroring is projecting onto another, that which you yourself are guilty of doing. In the speech below a US President lays out an argument for war. Interestingly, it is an argument for war against a country that has not attacked another country for over 150 years. Which US President do you think made the statement below?

> "Iran's leaders sow chaos, death, and destruction. They do not respect their neighbors' borders or the sovereign rights of nations. Instead Iran's leaders plunder the nation's resources to enrich themselves and to spread mayhem across the Middle East and far beyond."

Contrarily, when the US President Donald Trump made this statement, the US was at war with Afghanistan, Iraq, and Syria. Libya had been destroyed by the US and allied forces. Ukraine was also at war with US funding, training, logistical, and direct support, against Ukraine's own citizens, initially. And Taiwan was being garrisoned with increasing numbers of US 'trainers' and arms (see

Vietnam). The sovereign borders of multiple countries were being violated by the US and allied forces. And regarding the US's natural resources, they have long been plundered by an elite few, who had enriched themselves to the detriment of the 99% or We the People. The above is a textbook case of mirroring.

Your life, your parents' lives before you, and most possibly your grandparents' lives, have all been, in a way, hollowed out by war. Since the mid to late 1970s as a direct result of the now permanent war machine, the rise of inflation has been exponential. You have, in fact, been living on the exponential growth curve of inflation. You could compare it to living on an incredibly steep and treacherous street (there are a few of these in San Francisco). After decades of this you take it all in your stride, and even though a flat or flatter street would improve your daily life, you remain put and take it for normal. Whereas in fact living on this exponential growth curve has resulted in the buying power of the US dollar being reduced to pennies. But this is taken for normal.

Further, war serves as a triple threat to this 'Earth' and the various 'species' upon it and yet only a few are even vaguely familiar of this. War is death, it is financial ruination, and should 'climate change' be real, then it would be the biggest catalyst for 'climate change' that there is. War, in this respect, is uniquely intertwined with the many maladies from which we suffer, but not a voice is raised among governments, nor their media, nor those who advocate against 'climate change'. Even the voice of the 'antiwar' movement has gone scarce and quiet.

For all who now live, war, death, and destruction have been as constant as the air, the rising and setting of the sun, the rotation of this 'planet.' Whether asleep or awake war is and has been ever present. What is the most important aspect of war above all others and a prized necessity in the 'world' in which we 'live'? It is Inflation, of course.

## WAR & THE ECONOMY

What you may not realize is how closely war is tied to the financial and economic wellbeing of a country through inflation. In fact, war is inflationary, it is inflation.

I had thought to research and write a section about wealth distribution and equality in the US as part of this book. But what I found through my research was that little needed to be said about wealth distribution and equality that did not involve war, directly.

The economic casualties and the winners of war are all around us. The growing homeless and their encampments, the ever-increasing prices of homes and apartment rentals, the increasing prices of food, gas, education, and heating, the quickly deteriorating health and wellbeing of the citizens, the list goes on. The economic winners of war are the banks, the military industrial complex (MIC), the growing list of billionaires tied either directly or indirectly to the MIC, and those members of congress who support them. Further, even as their wealth increases each year, the billionaires and their corporations pay little if no tax at all. All of which points are directly tied to inflation.

The best way to spell it all out, comes from an animated story, an episode on the Peak Prosperity website[4]. This episode speaks to what we, the 99%, have collectively lost via all-the-time war and a rather traitorous earlier act.

The episode is Chapter 11: Inflation[5] and is part of the Peak Prosperity *The Crash Course* series. This chapter tells a succinct and powerful story of the why or, at least, part of the why of where we are. It begins with a graph that spans the years 1665 to 2013. Its axes are 'Price Level' and 'Year'.

What is immediately understood is that from the year 1665 to 1776 there was zero inflation. That is to say that what you purchased in 1665, cost the same in 1776, over 111 years later. So, that $0.15 loaf of bread that someone's great grandfather had purchased as a child or that $0.02 candy bar would both still cost the same and be of the same size, weight, and quantity 111 years later. Imagine what your parents or grandparents paid for their home 60, 70, 80 years ago, in the light of zero inflation. It

---

[4] Peak Prosterity https://peakprosperity.com/

[5] McKeon, A. (2021, September 10). *Chapter 11: Inflation*. Retrieved November 5, 2024, from https://peakprosperity.com/courses/crashcourse/lessons/crash-course-chapter-11-inflation/

would be the exact same price that you'd pay for a home today. Imagine that.

Understand that the only thing that temporarily disrupted what would have been a 195 years of zero inflation were wars—Revolutionary War (1776), War of 1808, Civil War (1861), World War I (1914-1918). These wars caused temporary hikes in prices, but shortly returned to baseline—zero inflation—after the war had subsided. Which is to say that for a full 195 years—1665 to 1842—a dollar was a dollar and your great, great grandfather's home would be the price that you would pay for a home today, 195 years later or thereabouts, with zero inflation.

The end of World War II changed everything. After all previous wars, there would be a dismantling of the war economy, a demobilization, all would return home, and the gold standard would once again underpin the nation's economy.

However, shortly after the end of World War II the gold standard was not readopted. Instead, it was replaced by a fiat currency that was administered by the Federal Reserve (below). Secondly, there was no dismantling of what had been the war economy, nor was there a demobilization. Instead the Pentagon was formed on September 18, 1947, which instituted continuous war spending and full mobilization. Additionally, a decades long cold war was waged, which sent military spending skyrocketing. The result of the preceding measures began the rapid, exponential rise of inflation, that as mentioned above, we live with and experience today as well as the monstrous US debt which is a direct result.

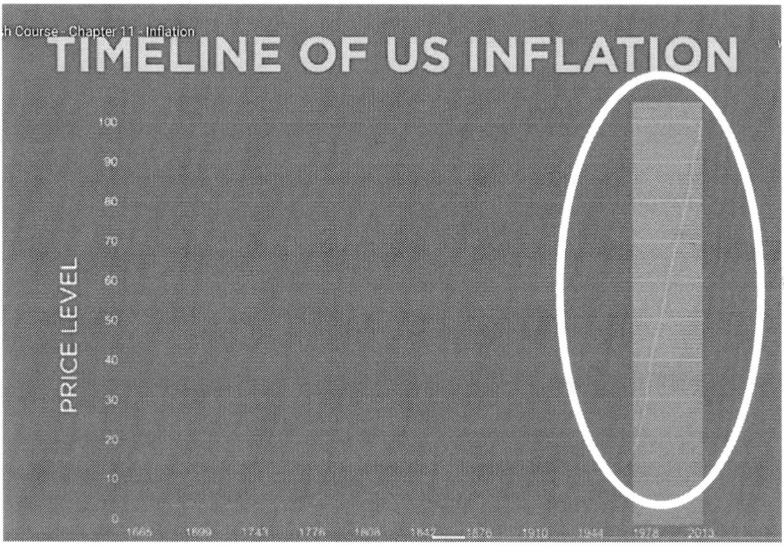


The most critical takeaway from the Chapter 11: "Inflation" episode of *The Crash Course* was that wars are, by their nature, inflationary. And that the inflation that we all currently suffer is a purposely engineered outcome. Inflation is a wealth transfer mechanism that concentrates wealth. Inflation is not a mistake, it is, again, a purposed mechanism with an incredibly destructive nature.

What we now have, has been the policy directive of every governmental administration from the end of World War II to the present. War continues unabated to date, for the reasons of sustained inflation, the concentration of wealth and the impoverishment of the masses, the 99%. What you suffer when purchasing food, utilities, gas, etc. and what the growing homeless have suffered is intrinsically tied to the sustained inflation of war. That you work in a job that is barely able to keep you afloat, and that you are one to two paychecks away from financial implosion is also due to the inflation of war. Now it takes two salaries in an attempt to maintain a household where before the inflationary-war spending paradigm took over it took just one. In fact, since the late 1970s we have all been living on an exponential-inflation growth curve as shown in the image above[6] (white oval).

The result is the greatest disparity in wealth between rich and poor for over 100 years, if not ever. And again, the primary beneficiaries of such a paradigm are banks, the military contractors, the corporations, oligarchs, and the politicians and government officials, who are paid/bribed by them.

That traitorous earlier act, referred to above, was the December 23, 1913 Federal Reserve Act[7]. Senate democrats, still in congress during Christmas recess and thus in the majority, passed the bill which President Woodrow Wilson signed. The majority of Senators, however, were home with their families when the traitorous act was passed. This act gave another entity—the Federal Reserve, a private banking concern—the right to print money for the

---

[6] McKeon, A. (2021, September 10). *Chapter 11: Inflation*. Retrieved November 5, 2024, from https://peakprosperity.com/courses/crashcourse/lessons/crash-course-chapter-11-inflation/

[7] The United States Senate (n.d.). *The Senate Passes the Federal Reserve Act*. Retrieved December 6, 2024, from https://www.senate.gov/artandhistory/history/minute/Senate_Passes_the_Federal_Reserve_Act.htm

US government and to charge it with interest. Thus the US government would need to borrow money from the Federal Reserve and pay it interest for something it could have done interest free.

What we have lost for turning over the US government's responsibility to print its own money free of interest, is no less than the country's true economic and financial freedom. Why would a government give up its right to print all the money that it needs, free of interest, and hand it over to another concern that would charge it interest to do the same thing?

President Woodrow Wilson realized much too late that what he had done would forever cripple the actual potential of the US. And it would also saddle the nation with monstrous future debt (as of 12/06/2024: $36.2 trillion US debt[8]). Understand that had the Federal Reserve Act not been signed into law, this debt would be a fraction of a fraction of what it is, if not equal to zero (0). Further, the government could have easily issued a mere 1%

---

[8] US Debt Clock (n.d.). *US Debt Clock*. Retrieved December 6, 2024, from https://usdebtclock.org/

interest for money that it had created and then loaned, which would have resulted in a positive balance.

> "I am a most unhappy man. I have unwittingly ruined my country. A great industrial nation is now controlled by its system of credit.
>
> We are no longer a government of free opinion, no longer a government by conviction and the vote of the majority, but a government by the opinion and duress of a small group of dominant men"[9].
>
> —Woodrow Wilson, 9/25/1919

The mistake for which Woodrow Wilson had apologized, today impacts on every family, every person in the US, and on their quality of 'life'. I have to imagine that any who voted for the Federal Reserve Act of 1913 would scarce believe what its future repercussions would be – or, then again, perhaps, not.

---

9 Russo, A. (Producer). (2006). *America: Freedom to Fascism* [Film]. Aaron Russo.

## WAR & CLIMATE CHANGE?

I was for a good long time a believer in 'global warming' which has since morphed into 'climate change'. And then, slowly, it happened. A clarity began to dawn, as dates for world destruction, premised on climate change, were all consecutively missed. These dates for destruction were then pushed farther into the future and new alarms were sounded and they too were missed. Then those who I had thought were independent purveyors of truth, were found not to be so independent after all and their 'truths' not to be truths at all. I sat with this for a while and began to see the game behind it all. It was not unlike the Project for A New American Century's (PNACs) "New Pearl Harbor"[10] as referenced in *Rebuilding America's Defenses: Strategies, Forces, and Resources For a New Century.*[11] It was written September 1, 2000, to, in short, impose America's will on the world (see Middle East). One

---

[10] Project for the New American Century. (2024, September 15). In *Wikipedia*. https://en.wikipedia.org/wiki/Project_for_the_New_American_Century

[11] Internet Archive (2000, September 1). *Rebuilding Americas Defenses*. Retrieved October 28, 2024, from https://archive.org/details/RebuildingAmericasDefenses

year and 10 days later, on September 11, 2001, three steel-framed buildings fell due to 'fire'. It would be the first time in history that a steel-framed building collapsed from fire, before or since. Was this PNAC's "New Pearl Harbor"? Question. Does fire pulverize concrete? Does fire eject multi-ton, steel girders several hundred feet away? Does fire cut steel girders at an angle? Or do you believe that it was Saudis armed with box cutters who outwitted the multi-trillion dollar US defense, security, and intelligence apparatus?

Subsequent to this "New Pearl Harbor", wars were precipitated across the Middle East, as outlined in the PNAC's own documents. Shortly thereafter, Saddam Hussein and Osama Bin Laden would be declared best friends for life and responsible for 9/11, while Weapons of Mass Destruction (WMD) would be reported to be in Iraq, somewhere. However, soon after Iraq was attacked and destroyed, all claims of WMD proved false. There were other claims for which other countries were attacked and they too were false. Though, as related to the prior section, the inflationary-war spending paradigm was pressing forward. But I digress.

'Global warming' or 'climate change', which we have been threatened with since the 1970s, had not rent the 'Earth' asunder, as I realized, despite all prior prognostications. Nor is there the likelihood that it will without the concerted and ongoing efforts of geoengineering to make it so. The skies above are replete with the sprayed, criss-cross tags of that handiwork. And even now there are those who deny this undeniable truth. Perhaps they simply refuse to look up.

I once thought such people simply mad or loyal to the status quo via payoff, or just willing deniers and/or completely subsumed by the system. Though I have discovered another very real possibility, which most will find shocking in the extreme, if not wholly unbelievable. That I will discuss in more detail in the following chapters.

What I also came to notice with regard to 'global warming' cum 'climate change' was that the 'movers and shakers', who had long championed 'climate change', were amassing ever greater wealth! Further, wouldn't 'climate change' be anathema to those beachfront homes that these 'movers and shakers' were buying up willy nilly? We'd been told that shorelines were sure to be eaten away due to melting ice and rising seas. Nonetheless, the 'movers and shakers' continued to grab up beachfront property and even beachfront properties on islands in the middle of the Pacific! 'Climate change' as we've long been lectured about would also see those very same islands submerged. Unless, of course, they were not being entirely honest with us, something there is unfortunately much precedence for. Then there were the jets of the 'movers and shakers' traversing the world, not just to 'climate change' forums and conferences. It's also quite difficult to forget those gluttonous, meat-loaded banquets, replete with all the things We the 'People' shouldn't eat, due to 'climate change'. Nonetheless, such foods were par for the course for the 'movers and shakers' and at 'climate change' forums and conferences too! Could there be a more obvious, collective b@*ch-slap across the face by them to the world, to their legion of dedicated, 'climate change' activists, and to their media spokespeople? No. It is as though the aim were to do such things, things that are anathema to their stated goals, in-plain-sight and particularly at 'climate change' forums/conferences. Why this flaunting by the 'movers and shakers' of their meat-loaded banquets and private jets? The synthesis which emerges is: "Do as I say, not as I do. I have profits to consider".

I then began to see something in the rooms of the various climate change gangs, figuratively speaking. It was something that could not be denied, nor unseen once seen, nor could it be avoided. And it was loud too. This was the 50-foot tall, neon-red, trumpeting war elephant in their various rooms. It was in the rooms of government officials, world 'leaders', NGOs for 'climate change', 'climate change organizations/ activists, etc. Not even the  movers and shakers' gluttonous, meat-loaded banquets or their personal jets criss-crossing the world could compare to this elephant. But they, 'movers and shakers, could not see, nor could they hear this elephant of war.

No, as they wrung their hands with regard to the deplorable environmental crisis of 'climate change', they could not or, perhaps, refused to see the elephant. But perhaps eye avoidance of the beast, covering their ears when it trumpeted, and gracefully dancing around it, proved sufficient for their 'climate change' agenda and the attendant get-rich work to continue. *Cirque du Soleil* is, no doubt, quite jealous of their nifty, acrobatic dance moves. Perhaps they are waiting until the cows that they have slaughtered (and possibly eaten) or seek to slaughter to abate 'climate change', have come home.

Seeing through the clouds of obfuscation and lies, the misdirection, the avoidance of the glaringly obvious, and one of the most potent brainwashing, cult-programming events ever, was to see that 'climate change' was not real. It was and has always been solely for profit and control. They know well and see clearly the war elephant in the room. Of course they do. It is, after all, their pet war elephant, which they feed and walk continuously.

Understand that these 'climate change' leaders are in direct support of the most obvious, pernicious, and aggressive form of 'climate change'—war—that ever there was. And it is dichotomous in the extreme to pursue 'climate change' initiatives as war rages and continues to rage unabated. It is only when the tiniest species of either red or black ants can leap over the Empire State Building in a single bound, that war will end – or that the world will end of 'climate change' (without geoengineering). Yet, the 'climate change' congregation bows its head and marches forward oblivious to this perverse and distractingly obvious contradiction.

It is possible that climate change organizations/ activists and their supporters, who sit in front of fire engines and ambulances, who defile great works of art, and perpetrate various other forms of civil disobedience are MKULTRA'd. Perhaps, in this way they have become members of a cult unable to even see the glaringly obvious 50-foot tall, neon-red, trumpeting war elephant.

There are even Green parties across the world, who are diametrically opposed to their own party platforms and who encourage war. One Green party, in particular, the German Green party, has walked the streets in military fatigues in favor of war.

> "A green party is a formally organized political party based on the principles of green politics, such as environmentalism and social justice. Green party platforms typically embrace social

> democratic economic policies and form coalitions with other left-wing parties."[12]

The German government's Green Party's ministers Robert Habeck and Foreign Minister Annalena Baerbock have, apparently, never met a war that they didn't like or chose not to support. Given the fact that wars and militaries are, again, the main cause of 'climate change' does this not represent the antithesis of Green party philosophy?

Nonetheless, these two green party officials and ministers serving in Germany's ruling coalition government may well be amongst the most pro-war ministers in Western Europe. Scratching your head yet?

These Green party officials pledge their fealty via billions of dollars of continued support and weaponry and act against the wishes of the very people who voted them into office, often with disdain. They have visited and assured warring nations of their support. And an icon of the 'climate

---

[12] Wikipedia (n.d.). *Green party*. https://en.wikipedia.org/wiki/Green_party

change' cadre, did herself visit one of the warring nations and appeared to pledge fealty to it. Is there not both great irony and great contradiction in this move? Is it not antithetical to the cause of those who purport to be 'climate change' activists?

There is not a governmental voice raised across the whole of Western Europe, North America, New Zealand and Australia against these wars. They are, in fact, all participating in these wars, which rage. They send or 'loan' billions of dollars of equipment. They send 'advisers', who might 'occasionally' engage in combat. These same 'advisers' might also, 'occasionally', man missile batteries and howitzers, drive tanks and other armored vehicles, and program missiles for deep strikes into the territory of its nuclear-armed adversary.

Those still possessed of some small critical thinking ability or some remaining degree of common sense, and who call themselves 'Green' or 'Climate Activist' or 'Environmentalist', must understand the inherent contradiction here. Governments wield strict penalties against citizens who violate carbon initiatives, drive their older, unregistered cars, and against farmers the world over, who raise cattle and other livestock, and are told to end this due to 'climate change'. But what about war?

All is quiet on the Western front and in 'climate change' communities, with government leaders, the leaders of world bodies, climate change activists, and attendant organizations, NGOs, etc., dancing around the 50-foot tall, neon-red, trumpeting war elephant that goes unseen and unheard. This as war spending reaches an all time high of over $4.5 trillion a year worldwide. Go figure.

As of the writing of this book, The Global Climate Intelligence Group's World Climate Declaration states clearly that There is No Climate Emergency. (https://clintel.org/world-climate-declaration/). The 1,971 signatories to the World Climate Declaration, are scientists, engineers, and other experts in over 64 countries. Contrary to the movers and shakers they have no profits to make, no political agendas, no beach front homes to purchase. Who do you believe?

## THE GOVERNMENT, ETC.

The musical chairs dance of a rotating government with this frontman or frontwoman for 'high office' and that continues to gin up a loyalty and devotion which can scarce be believed. This in the face of monstrous incompetence, obvious mental illness, ongoing criminality, narcissism, sociopathy, and psychopathy that are perpetually in play. And at this very moment, the deceit is so pervasive and so obvious, that in a sane society those responsible would be banished to the edges of that society, at the very least. However, in this society it is not so. Why?

It is a direct result of the people who are drawn into politics, for whom politics allows them to be fully themselves. These people are not out to serve the public, not out to improve the lives of citizens, not out to maintain and safeguard the public commons or their trust. They are merely taking orders. And it takes but a few simple questions to see the truth of this.

Has life gotten better for you and those of your generation, since you've been voting? Has life gotten better, collectively, for your children or your grandchildren? Has the economic situation improved in the US? Has education improved? Has the country's infrastructure—roads, bridges, schools, parks, subways systems, public buildings, etc.—improved? Has inflation rebounded to the time of your youth or earlier (see War and the Economy)? No, they have not and demonstrably so.

These individuals who attain high office are no more than order takers, courtiers to power and money, political prostitutes. Search out their funders and you will find their client lists, their true constituents. And with great assurance I can tell you that We the People, the 99%, are not on these lists and therefore not taken into consideration. There will be the promises and the platitudes to assure you otherwise from those vying for office or in office during an election cycle. But how often are their promises put into practice?

To believe in government, to vote, in this day and age, and to expect that things will get better after decades of things, actually, getting worse, across the board, is to be too detached from reality and the truth on the ground.

Despite this very clear continual result, the indignation, rage, and hatred that one side—Red, Blue—feels for the other side and its candidate is palpable. And the joy experienced upon one side's victory seems euphoric. That is until the truth sets in and business proceeds as usual, and those pesky campaign promises are flushed away like the fetid refuse that they are.

How then to explain the indignation, rage, and hatred that one side feels for another? I would posit cradle-to-grave brainwashing/cult-programming and either willful or catastrophic ignorance. We've all seen this dance before and it ends the same way every time regardless of the dance team selected.

The nearly two years of orchestrated hate from the populace for this candidate or that is undergirded by a vaudevillian presidential marketing campaign, presented as though it were a television series. The candidates know exactly who they are working for. And in the words of the late George Carlin, "It ain't you." They are merely actors, with only the least capable, the most incompetent, the most inured to true power, and the most obedient selected to 'run'. They vie for their five minutes of fame and enduring wealth thereafter.

At the highest levels of government, once these politicians—presidents, vice presidents, cabinet members, etc.—serve their purpose, leave office, they become incredibly wealthy. There are the exorbitant speaking fees, board seats, 'consulting fees', private high-paying positions, and other forms of remuneration. It is their reward. And in their wake lie every unfulfilled campaign promise, every promise in office ever made, and a nation suffering exponential inflation and in ever-greater decay. Do you understand?

What is this called, when what the people vote for and want never comes to pass? It's called an Oligarchy, at best, not a Democracy. And though this is probably pretty obvious to most, it is only now becoming fashionable for professors to say such things openly. Though there are still those professors, who more often than not couched their findings with terms like, "further study is needed for a definite characterization". Really? The professors of political science at Northwestern University, Jeffery A. Winters and Benjamin I. Page, to their credit, used no such language, when they called the US an Oligarchy.

> "There is widespread agreement that the United States is a democracy. But is it possible that the US political system is also oligarchic? We believe that the concept of oligarchy can be fruitfully applied not only to places like Singapore, Colombia, Russia, and Indonesia, but also to the contemporary United States"[13].

The professors do, however, use less direct language when it comes to greater specificity with regard to who those oligarchs are, the type of influence that they have, whether they work in networks, and what policy areas they dominate, etc. Really? One imagines that it would be fairly easy to ascertain the answers to these questions, which could not be more obvious. One would suggest to the professors to look at the funding sources for the various politicians and government officials, and then the resulting 'legislation' and the 'tax breaks' as well. I imagine

[13] Winters, J. A., & Page, B. I. (2007). Oligarchy in the United States? *Academia*, 7(4). https://doi.org/:10.1017/S1537592709991770

that even these first steps would yield a good bit of information.

As I write, Donald Trump has again become president. Know that nothing will change as the system is hardwired and long ago secured against real change. The fate of John F. Kennedy was a warning and not a president since has stepped outside the lines or sought to fundamentally change things. What John F. Kennedy did not understand was that he was without true power. And that those with the power saw him as just a person, a 'human being', who happened to be a president. Thus he was a person for whom there was no regard.

Those elected to high office, truly, have no power. So little power do they have, that they could not enact or make true the least of their campaign promises even if they wished to do so. But know, as a matter of fact, that they do not.

When you think of your wellbeing, perhaps start by asking someone who has suffered through a recent catastrophic event—Hurricane Helene, Hurricane Katrina. There is no doubt that their experience would be up close and personal and very reflective of the times. Especially when the agency charged with helping them — Federal Emergency Management Association (FEMA) — has been inverted into a grift. A grift that steals, hoards funds designated for emergencies, stops others from helping those who have been through devastating emergencies and then shows up Johnny-come-lately and does nothing. Or it complains about the fact that it is being criticized for having done nothing, while offering embarrassing amounts of relief ($700, $750) to those who have lost, literally, everything. Then, tragically, FEMA denies those who seek the incredibly minuscule relief offered, when they do apply for it! Grift?! You are here.

## THE CABAL-BELOW

In this chapter everything that precedes this section and that comes after it is connected to the cabal-below.

Know that your government is beholden, entirely, to those who I will refer to as the cabal-below. Who makes up this cabal? The cabal-below, as I will call them, are, by and large, very old money. Some would scarce believe how old and how long some of them have been around. These older 'families' would make other cabal-below members—the Rothchilds, the Morgans, the Rockefellers, etc.—seem as though newborns. They are the 'quiet' deep in the background, who disdain the spotlight and attention. One imagines a millennia or two in the spotlight will destroy one's diet for it.

The wealth of the cabal is not measured in tens or hundreds of billions of dollars. These are the kind of sums that their subjugates might amass over 20, 30, 40 years, or even a century. Understand, those in the topmost portion of the cabal-below's pyramid have been in power for centuries if not millennia, transferring their wealth from empire to empire. One has but to witness the UK's royal family, whose true wealth is, no doubt, a great secret, to understand succession and continued wealth accumulation. The royal family's wealth has not diminished, in fact, it has grown, despite their empire's fall. Now imagine much, much older families, who have been amassing wealth for, again, centuries, if not millennia. Any such family meeting the least of this timeline and not having amassed tens if not hundreds of trillions of dollars, would represent the height of financial malfeasance and mismanagement. Doubtless some of the families have succumbed to this, but those who continue on meet the threshold of tens of trillions of dollars, at the very least. Understand that this provides them with the ability to buy countries, and, in fact, anyone who is bereft of any degree of integrity. Those who do still maintain any degree of integrity lie as near to extinction as the very last Dodo bird in the present 'world'. It is these people, the cabal-below, who are the overlords of this 'earthly' paradigm. But even they are beholden to others.

As per the quote from George Carlin at the start of this chapter, your government was purchased, bought and sold a long time ago. What you have now is interchangeable front people, who serve their time in office, and follow the dictates that come from the unelected far above them—the cabal-above. They will spend your tax dollars as commanded to, first and foremost on war, and on agendas, which serve the cabal's best interest—climate change initiatives, carbon credits, tax cuts, etc. And they will do so while taking the country apart piece by piece and parceling it out as the cabal-below sees fit (see Manufacturing Infrastructure, China). Voting, in this respect, could not be more of a farce, the rigged game that it currently is.

The monstrous farce of politics and the hamster-wheel belief that participation in it elicits anything other than a momentary endorphin hit – or psychotic dread – as the country continues on its nightmarish decomposition, is true insanity. And, unfortunately, those who do still participate in the political process unknowingly march the rest of us towards a very inauspicious end. That end can be seen just over the hill—it is being called the great reset.

Those who actually rule and run your government—the cabal-below—are, of course, unelected. They do not rotate in and out of governmental positions. In addition to controlling your government and, perhaps, a main reason why your government is so susceptible to control, is because they control the printing of your national currency. In truth, this control encompasses all national currencies, West, East, and other. Got a central bank? Your national currency is controlled (see Brazil, Russia, India,

China, South Africa, etc). There are no independent countries, save the smallest—North Korea, Cuba, Iran—possibly, who have yet to be overthrown. Thus the wailing and wringing of hands, the gnashing of teeth regarding these 'evil' countries, who, to a one, have not attacked another country in decades or even centuries (see Iran).

Further, their plans, long established, are the overriding structures and framework, which your governments must meet—perpetual war, 'climate change' initiatives, carbon credits, 'smart' everything, COVID-19, 15-minute cites, great reset, and a digital currency to rule over them all.

It does make one wonder about the continuity, not of empires, but of their oligarchs and the ruling structures behind the various thrones. Did these too go extinct along with their empires? Or did they simply move their funds and themselves to the latest empire of note? There is little doubt that their financial wherewithal would, in time, ingratiate them into controlling circles, find them befriended among the powerful, and soon in control once again. Having seen up close how an empire works from the inside would provide a formidable advantage.

To take the demise of the most recent empire, the British Empire (16th-20th Century) as an example. Its oligarchs, banking families, the financial powers seated in the City of London, and certainly its royalty have endured on and even now expand their control (see great reset). To look into their deep ancestry would, perhaps, provide more than a few clues to imperial or, at least, oligarchic and moneyed continuity.

This is no more than a long-winded way of saying that from the motley presidents and prime ministers and politicians to the oligarchs/organizations (small, large, public, hidden), to the banking clans, to those who sit atop the pyramid, these people are not your friends. They do not care for you or yours, and to rise to such levels, it appears that one must be bereft, entirely, of compassion and empathy, and well along the spectrum which begins at narcissist (see 'COVID-19, Democide). Please stop voting for their front people. You are here.

## SECTION TWO

### 'Earth': 'Healthcare?'

"The materials masquerading as vaccines were designed intentionally to harm the people who received them".

—Dr. Michael Yeadon

**Allopathy** (noun): al-lop-a-thy | ə-läp-ə-thē:
a system of medical practice that aims to combat disease by use of remedies (drugs or surgery) producing effects different from or incompatible with those produced by the disease being treated. (May 2022 definition)

**Allopathy** (noun): al-lop-a-thy | ə-läp-ə-thē:
a system of medical practice that emphasizes diagnosing and treating disease and the use of conventional, evidence-based therapeutic measures (such as drugs or surgery). (November 2022 definition)[14]

[14] Medicine: The Killing Fields, Dr. Sam Bailey: https://odysee.com/@drsambailey:c/Medicine-The-Killing-Fields:1

Allopathic medicine is the predominant form of medicine practiced in the US, as initially defined above in the first definition and then subsequently changed in the second. The new definition seeks to up the validity of allopathic medicine, which references the 'motto' of "evidence-based medicine", a definition which became very popular during the 'pandemic'. Its ally, "follow the science", was also readily deployed during the 'pandemic'.

For the last several years, at least, Iatrogenesis[15]— [Allopathic] medical error leading to death induced by a physician's words or therapy— has been the third leading cause of death in the US. But as of 2023, perhaps even earlier, Iatrogenesis was suddenly completely absent from the list. Firstly, there is both great irony and great tragedy of a 'medical system' which represents a country's third leading cause of death. However, given the allopathic 'curatives'— ventilator, Remdisiver, Midazolam/morphine cocktail, 'COVID-19 vaccines', etc.—employed during the 'pandemic' and the resulting deaths, it is entirely possible that Iatrogenesis is no longer the third leading causes of death. In fact, it may well have

---

[15] Medical error — the third leading cause of death in the US

reached the first, if not the second leading cause of death. I imagine that its absence from the list is just temporary, an oversight.

It was quite odd that the various search engines did not bring up, nor did they list Iatrogenesis as a leading cause of death in 2023. Number three was, in some cases, simply listed as "Accidents/Unintentional Injuries."[16] Was this Iatrogenesis in disguise? Perhaps the public healthcare system now abstains from telling this most damaging truth about itself. This finds a parallel in the way that all types of the flu have either disappeared or morphed into 'COVID-19'. Or these are both temporary oversights, soon to be corrected, and the various seasonal flus will reappear.

We have all just gone through what may or may not be called, at a later time, a world democide, as this term reflects exactly what has occurred and continues to this day. Though many have deemed it a flu 'pandemic', this it never was. Flus, being upper respiratory infections, have never caused turbo cancers, myocarditis, pericarditis, thrombosis, strokes,

---

[16] US News & World Report Top 10 Causes of Death in America

Sudden Adult Deaths (SADS), menstrual dysregulation, MS, Guillain Barre, Bell's Palsy, sterility, etc. That would be the work of a toxic substance or, more specifically, a biotoxin designed to send one's various systems into dysregulation. That said, this toxic substance or biotoxin also had a second and a tertiary purpose, which the mainstream media have completely ignored. But more on that later.

While I have only touched lightly upon the topic of politics, it is critically necessary to have a sober and yet a compassionate look at what has and continues to happen via the recent 'COVID-19 pandemic'. Literally billions of people across the world have been lied to in a coordinated campaign that involved world governments, world public and private healthcare organizations, the media, academia, the scientific community, high tech, etc. The result is that people across the world have been seriously injured, disabled, serially murdered, or become, with all due respect, the walking dead. The numbers may well approach World War II casualty numbers (if they haven't already).

The evidence of this, despite the raging lockstep censorship campaign, is all around you. It is in the excess deaths that insurance companies know exist and lament, as they will have to pay the costs. It is in skyrocketing cancers and turbo cancers, and normal, healthy athletes and non-athletes suddenly dropping dead in record numbers. It is in children having heart attacks and developing myocarditis, pericarditis, thrombosis, etc. Let me repeat that: children are having heart attacks. It is in the working young, mandated to take the vaccine, who have died and are dying in higher numbers than the old.[17] These working-age Millennials have experienced a "Vietnam War death spike" as Edward Dowd calls it, in one year alone. It is in the 1.5 million adverse events from 'COVID-19 vaccines' reported to the government's Vaccine Adverse Events Reporting System (VAERS). This number represents more adverse events than all other vaccines combined over its 32 year history. And, even given all of the above adverse events, there are pages and pages more of adverse events uncovered in Pfizer's own documents.

---

[17] Edward Dowd Presents Irrefutable Evidence Vaccine Mandates Killed & Disabled Countless Americans: https://vigilantfox.news/p/edward-dowd-presents-irrefutable?utm_source=substack&utm_medium=email#play

These are the Pfizer documents that the FDA (Federal Drug Administration), in collaboration with Pfizer, tried to keep hidden for 75 years[18] from you. When does an agency purposed with protecting and promoting public health, conspire with an agency it is supposed to be protecting us from?

Why this lockstep banning and censorship of any and every piece of information that would throw a light on what is actually happening and not what you are being told is happening? Does this not on face value seem, well, nefarious, of ill intent? Are we not adults able to make our own decisions based on all the supplied information?

The above said, there are three topics of concern under this section of the book, as they are of extreme importance to us all. The topics are the current system of medicine, what has and is happening, as a result of the 'pandemic', and the masks, which we were initially told did not help and then told that they did.

---

[18] Wolf Dr , N. (2022, May 29). Dear Friends, Sorry to Announce a Genocide. Retrieved October 29, 2024, from https://naomiwolf.substack.com/p/dear-friends-sorry-to-announce-a?s=r

The deaths linked to the use of Remdesivir, (Midazolam UK) and the increased use of intubation by medical staffs,[19] the deaths resulting from turbo cancers, myocarditis, pericarditis, thrombosis, strokes, Sudden Adult Deaths (SADS), etc., can all be linked directly to allopathic care and the implementation of the 'COVID-19 vaccines'. Private and public health are astutely aware of this. There have been a number of clear indications that something was wrong. And temporally[20]—of or relating to the sequence of time—for those actually looking, the cause would have been easy to pin down—'COVID-19 vaccine' distribution. There can be little doubt that Iatrogenesis was destined for the top cause of death, the number one spot on the list as a result of this alone. And the data, the facts are continuing to mount.

---

[19] Olszewski, E. M. (2020). *Undercover Epicenter Nurse: How Fraud, Negligence, and Greed Led to Unnecessary Deaths at Elmhurst Hospital* (1st ed.). Hot Books. https://www.amazon.com/Undercover-Epicenter-Nurse-Negligence-Unnecessary/dp/151076366X

[20] "Temporal." Merriam-Webster.com Dictionary, Merriam-Webster, https://www.merriam-webster.com/dictionary/temporal. Accessed 29 Dec. 2024.

As I had referred to earlier, a devastating discovery was made regarding those 25 to 64 years of age, comprising the country's working age population and mandated to receive the various COVID-19 vaccines, by the insurance company OneAmerica's CEO, Scott Davison. Davison's comment was related by Edward Dowd, former equity portfolio manager for Blackrock:

> "One America CEO Scott Davison, in a chamber of commerce meeting, revealed that he had seen 40% excess mortality in the millennial age group 25 through 64. He said that a 10% increase would be once in a 200-year-flood or three standard deviation event. 40% was off the charts."[21]

Yet, government officials, at all levels, public, private, and world healthcare officials/organizations, academia, scientists, the mainstream media, social media mavens, big tech avoid, evade, and dance nervously around the most probable cause of death —the 'COVID-19 vaccines'. Even Scott Davison with the temporally-aligned statics staring him in the face,

---

[21] "You Can't Hide the Dead Bodies" – Edward Dowd Testifies on Excess Deaths: https://vigilantnews.com/post/you-cant-hide-the-dead-bodies-edward-dowd-testifies-on-excess-deaths/

attributed the deaths to 'COVID-19'. Have you ever witnessed such inanity and blatant disregard for what is, no doubt, a highly probable cause of death, disease, and illness—the 'COVID-19 vaccines'?

To date, the 'COVID-19 vaccine's' inclusion in any investigation has been absent, entirely. This is a clear sign that there was awareness of what was happening, followed by fear and desperation that it was being found out. Perhaps the insurance 'angle' was one that they had not anticipated. In a sane and principled world, the 'COVID-19- vaccines' would have been listed as the cause of death. And as the CDC's own graph shows, when the 'COVID-19 vaccines' were mandated and 'rolled out' to the general public and to companies of over 100 employees, where Millennials were heavily represented, Millennial excess deaths skyrocketed. This would be the part being played by allopathic medicine, per the new definition 11/22, which prescribes the use of conventional, evidence-based therapeutic measures to treat disease, in this case the 'COVID-19 vaccines'. Interestingly, the 'COVID-19 vaccines' were not at all conventional, and the actual evidence on them was incredibly thin, as many trials had either not been undertaken, or were stopped short of being completed. And there were some instances too where many of the participants' files or data was 'lost'. As for being therapeutic measures, one only need look at the 1.5 million adverse events reported to VAERS to judge the truth of this.

**Exhibit 4 | Millenials Suffered Rapid and Record Rate of Excess Deaths in Fall '21**

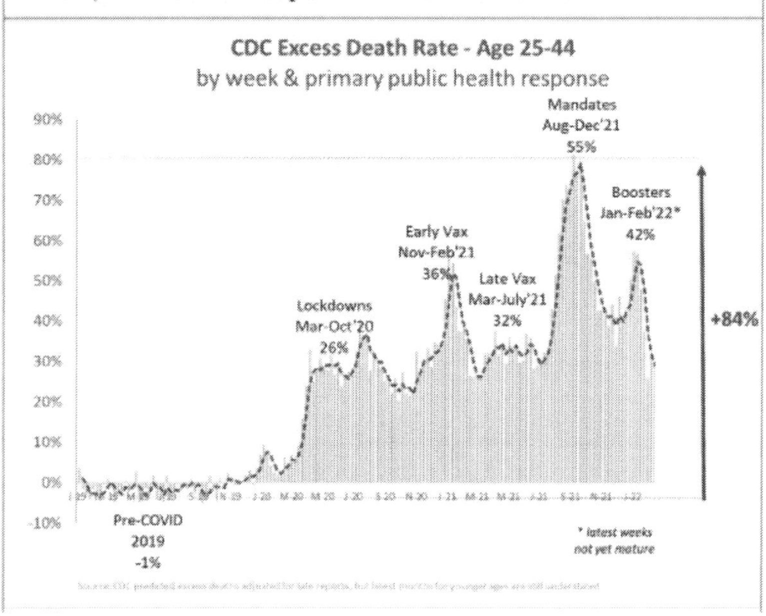


The graph shows the pre-'COVID-19' period in 2019, the onset of Lockdowns (Mar-Oct '20), Early Vaccination (Nov-Feb '21), Late Vaccination (Mar-July '21), Mandates (Aug-Dec '21), and Boosters (Jan-Feb

'22). From what had been normal in 2019 to the onset of lockdowns, vaccinations, and subsequent booster shots, excess death of the 25-44 age group, millennials increased by 84%. Yet, the same coterie of 'officials' fumble around in a lighted room, as though they were in the dark, avoiding, at all cost, the neon yellow elephant trumpeting loudly in the same room. Edward Dowd, responsible for detailing this graph along with his colleagues, had this to say:

> "Starting in the summer into the fall with the mandates and the boosters, there were 61,000 excess millennial deaths. Basically, millennials experienced a Vietnam War in the second half of 2021…This is what we call democide, death by government."[22]
>
> —Edward Dowd

The continued avoidance of the 'COVID-19 vaccines' as directly causative, thus directly responsible for the increase in all case excess mortality rate in the US must constitute criminal negligence. How can it not?

---

[22] Edward Dowd Presents Irrefutable Evidence Vaccine Mandates Killed & Disabled Countless Americans: https://vigilantfox.news/p/edward-dowd-presents-irrefutable?utm_source=substack&utm_medium=email#play

> "Criminal negligence refers to conduct in which a person ignores a known or obvious risk, or disregards the life and safety of others"
>
> —Shouse Law Group[23]

This neon yellow elephant continues to trumpet in the many rooms of government officials, healthcare officials/organizations, attendant academicians, scientists, the mainstream media, social media, high-tech, and others. As a result they have also become skilled avoidance acrobats on a parallel level with *Cirque du Soleil* (see Neon Red Elephants) for their determination to avoid, at all costs, the obvious —'COVID-19 vaccines' as cause of death and mounting adverse events.

Of course, via Occam's razor the simplest determination would be to seek out what happened from a temporal perspective in parallel to the rising death toll. This is information that they currently have in their possession. It is a puzzle easily solved by an apt high school student. Though experienced researchers, investigators, scientists, pathologists,

---

[23] SHOUSE LAW GROUP: https://www.shouselaw.com/ca/defense/laws/criminal-negligence/

federal agencies cannot and will not make this determination. Integrity and honesty, it seems, have moved from the list of endangered species to the list of the extinct, in these circles, at least.

As one of Mr. Dowd researchers discovered, there has been a "mix shift in the age of death, since the roll out of the 'COVID-19 vaccines'". What this means is that the young and millennials, in particular, were dying more quickly than those over 65 years of age. Mr. Dowd's team further discovered that:

> "In 2020 there were 126,000 excess deaths under the age of 65, or approximately 21%. In year 2 of the Pandemic, there were 181,000 excess deaths of people under the age of 65, or approximately 35%. But millennials saw the most enormous increase: 45%, from 42,000 excess deaths to 61,000 excess deaths."

Mr. Dowd states in the brief quote above that the 61,000 deaths represented the total losses in the Vietnam war, a seven year period, but this death toll had happened in less than a year with Millennials. And yet, alarm bells are not ringing from coast to coast. Quite to the contrary, the dance of avoidance continues on with the 'COVID-19 vaccines' still available, despite their unparalleled record of adverse events. This could not be a more potent clue.

There is, yet, more damning information with regard to the public healthcare system and more compelling information for Iatrogenesis as the number one leading cause of death.

A recent study led by Oxford University's Professor Colm D. Andrews, involved 1.7 million children ages 5 to 15, who had received the Pfizer 'COVID-19 vaccine' and those who had not. The children who took part in the study were registered with the UK's National Healthcare System.

The study found that only children who had received the Pfizer 'COVID-19 vaccine' suffered myocarditis and pericarditis. However, there were no cases found in the children who had not been vaccinated—the unvaccinated group. To repeat, children who had not received the 'COVID-19 vaccine' did not suffer heart damage. It was also discovered that not a single child of the 1.7 million died from 'COVID-19'. Lastly, the study documented that the 'COVID-19 vaccines' offered little protection from the virus with many of the 'COVID-19 vaccinated' children being infected within 14 to 15 weeks after receiving the 'COVID-19' injection[24] [25]. In other words, 'COVID-19 vaccines' caused 'COVID-19'.

Lastly, the US Government's own Vaccine Adverse Event Reporting System (VAERS), wherein fewer that 1% of vaccine adverse events are reported, has discovered that there have been more adverse events reported for the 'COVID-19 vaccines', than all other vaccines combined over a 32 year period.[26] To date, VAERS has received nearly 1.5 million reports of adverse reactions and deaths associated with the 'COVID-19 vaccines'.[27] Any of the prior vaccines

---

[24] OpenSAFELY: Effectiveness of COVID-19 vaccination in children and adolescents: https://www.bennett.ox.ac.uk/papers/10.1101/2024.05.20.24306810/

[25] Study of 1.7 Million Children: Heart Damage Only Found in Covid-Vaxxed Kids: Frank Bergman October 7, 2024:

[26] *Cause Unknown": The Epidemic of Sudden Deaths in 2021 & 2022*, Edward Dowd: Kindle, pg. 131

[27] *Cause Unknown": The Epidemic of Sudden Deaths in 2021 & 2022*, Edward Dowd: Kindle, pg. 127

would have long been recalled from the market after such a result. Why weren't the 'COVID-19 vaccines'?

As to Iatrogenesis rising higher on the list of top causes of death, the VAERS information listed above may well be a pointer in that direction. The number of reported adverse events totaling 1.5 million contained within it thousands of deaths that occurred either on the same day as the 'COVID-19 vaccines' or within one to two days[28]. A simple extrapolation of VAERS own statement, that only one percent (1%) report adverse vaccine events, might well find unimaginable numbers of the 'COVID-19 vaccinated' who have not only adversely affected, but who have died as a direct result off the 'COVID-19 vaccines'.

It is both horrific and shocking to see the rising death toll among babies, children, working-age Millennials, fit and healthy athletes, and all others who had been mandated to take the 'COVID-19 vaccines'. However, the abject silence in the face of these unprecedented adverse events is even more

---

[28] *Cause Unknown": The Epidemic of Sudden Deaths in 2021 & 2022*, Edward Dowd: Kindle, pg. 132

horrific and shocking. The abject silence of government officials at all levels, public, private, and world healthcare officials/organizations, academia, scientists, doctors and nurses, the mainstream media, social media, big tech, etc., would seem to signal a collective awareness of an ongoing crime against 'humanity'. And 'cause unknown' is not a smoke screen, though they might wish it to be: it is, instead, the tacit awareness of what is and has been happening—crimes against 'humanity'. Thus with 1.5 million+ smoking guns in the government's own reporting system and excess deaths at multiples of baseline, a sane society would see the establishment of Nuremberg type courts for this egregious crime against 'humanity'. These numbers are, of course, but the tip of the iceberg, as only one percent of those affected report to VAERS. Imagine for a moment the actual numbers of the adversely affected and those who have been killed.

To date, several billion people have taken a 'COVID-19 vaccine' whose definition was changed in order that what was not previously a vaccine could be called such. Said 'COVID-19 vaccines' per the pharmaceutical companies' own documents state that, in many cases, it was not tested and its efficacy not proven. In fact several ingredients that have been divulged, a number still have not been, are known to be toxic.

> "The Food and Drug Administration is responsible for protecting the public health by ensuring the safety, efficacy, and security of human and veterinary drugs, biological products, and medical devices; and by ensuring the safety of our nation's food supply, cosmetics, and products that emit radiation."[29]

What governmental agency, in this case, the US Food and Drug Administration, charged with the responsibilities listed above, would seek to have a court keep secret from the public for 75 years 55,000 of Pfizer internal documents? These are documents for the 'COVID-19 vaccines', that have been killing, maiming, and/or disabling those to whom it is injected and VAERS is very clear on that. Why would the FDA do such a thing?

---

[29] US Food and Drug Administration (n.d.). *What We Do*. https://www.fda.gov/about-fda/what-we-do

Cannot any right thinking person, at least, see the action on the part of the FDA as dubious? And given the fact that the FDA had seen these documents, does this not reflect a conflict of interest, at best? The proof in Pfizer's own documents points to the fact that Pfizer's executives lied about the efficacy, the toxicity, and the contents of their 'COVID-19 vaccines'. Finally, they also lied about the fact that their vaccines would, in fact, cause 'COVID-19'!

> "Pfizer (and thus the FDA) knew by December 2020 that the MRNA vaccines did not work — that they "waned in efficacy" and presented "vaccine failure." One side effect of getting vaccinated, as they knew by one month after the mass 2020 rollout, was "COVID.""[30]
>
> — Dr. Naomi Wolfe, Outspoken

It becomes quite clear why further tests in light of Pfizer's own documents were not undertaken. And the FDA's knowledge of the Pfizer documents should be extremely troubling to all who have taken the Pfizer 'COVID-19 vaccination'.

---

[30] Wolf Dr., N. (2022, May 29). Dear Friends, Sorry to Announce a Genocide. Retrieved October 29, 2024, from https://naomiwolf.substack.com/p/dear-friends-sorry-to-announce-a?s=r

> "Pfizer skewed the trial subjects so that almost three quarters were female — a gender that is less prone to cardiac damage. Pfizer lost the records of what became of hundreds of their trial subjects.
>
> In the internal trials, there were over 42,000 adverse events and more than 1200 people died. Four of the people who died, died on the day they were injected."
>
> —Dr. Naomi Wolfe, Outspoken[31]

And with doctors and nurses, clinicians and pharmacists continuing, to this day, with all of the available evidence, to inject these toxic, injurious 'COVID-19 vaccines' to the public, the motto "Do no Harm" has been monstrously desecrated.

There were those medical professionals, who said "No" and who were fired from their jobs for not administering, nor taking an unproven, toxic 'vaccine' that was known to present "vaccine failure."

---

[31] Wolf Dr., N. (2022, May 29). "Dear Friends, Sorry to Announce a Genocide". Retrieved October 29, 2024, from https://naomiwolf.substack.com/p/dear-friends-sorry-to-announce-a?s=r

Another example of healthcare professionals standing together against forced vaccine mandates were the 100,000+ UK health practitioners of the UK's National Healthcare System, who were ready to quit because they knew first hand what was going on, though they were not fired because of the obvious implications[32].

The excess deaths and mounting disabilities from the mandates of the various vaccines can no longer be hidden. Nor can the acts of those who were knowingly complicit in crimes against humanity. Professionals who had a first hand perspective of the damage being done by the vaccines to babies, children, teenagers, young adults, pregnant mothers, and the balance of society.

What 'healthcare' system finds itself at the top of a nations' causes of death year after year and yet continues to call itself a 'healthcare' system? And it appears that when those deaths become far too

---

[32] Gregory, A. (2022, January 1). *Mandatory Covid jabs for healthcare workers in England to be scrapped*. Retrieved December 7, 2024, from https://amp.theguardian.com/politics/2022/mar/01/mandatory-covid-jabs-dropped-nhs-staff-england-march-health-social-care-workers-law-vaccinated-sajid-javid

numerous and the 'healthcare' system finds itself without peer or near peer in deaths each year, the related deaths—Iatrogenesis—simply go unlisted. And in this case something else, "Cause Unknown" takes its place. Think of "Cause Unknown" for a healthcare system that "follows the science". Where is their science in determining so many unknown causes of death as directly related to it? It is nowhere to be seen.

You are told none of the above, directly. In fact, you are told the direct opposite—"Safe and effective", "Flatten the curve", "Follow the science", and "Chemtrails is a conspiracy theory".

The above represents but a small discussion on the US Healthcare system or, more generally, the Medical Industrial Complex and those agencies charged with keeping that complex profitable at all costs.

eu·gen·ics (yo͞o-jĕn′ĭks)[33]n.: The study or practice of attempting to improve the human gene pool by encouraging the reproduction of people considered to have desirable traits and discouraging or preventing the reproduction of people considered to have undesirable traits.

Question. How does Bill Gates, a non-medical doctor, a non-scientists, a non-research professional, with deep pharmaceutical investments, who is one of the biggest donors to the World Health Organization (WHO) through the Bill and Melinda Gates Foundation 'predict' an coming pandemic? A pandemic, by the way, which will represent a very profitable opportunity and, possibly, a significant increase in the value of his vast pharmaceutical stock portfolio, for any mandated vaccine that is tied to that portfolio?

> "First we got population. The world today has 6.8 billion people. That's headed up to about 9 billion. Now if we do a really great job on new vaccines, health care, reproductive health

[33] For the American Heritage Dictionary definition: Eugenicists. (n.d.) American Heritage® Dictionary of the English Language, Fifth Edition. (2011). Retrieved October 28 2024 from https://www.thefreedictionary.com/Eugenicists

services, we lower that by perhaps 10 or 15 percent."[34]

—Bill Gates, TED2010 Conference

Firstly, does anyone not see a glaring problem with this statement relative to 'vaccines', 'healthcare' and 'reproductive health'? It speaks very directly to them being utilized, at the very least, to decimate—to kill every tenth person (10%)—the world's population. Is this not a form of raw, clearly spoken eugenics, crimes against humanity?

The 'COVID-19' pandemic would prove a boon for pharmaceutical companies and their investors with various pharmaceutical companies entering into secret contracts with countries across the world. These same contracts indemnified the pharmaceutical companies from any and all responsibilities for what would be virtually untested 'COVID-19 vaccines'. 'COVID-19 vaccines' that would not have been labeled 'vaccines' under the prior definition.

---

[34] TED (2010, February 1). Innovating to zero! Bill Gates | TED2010 • February 2010. Retrieved October 28, 2024, from https://www.ted.com/talks/bill_gates_innovating_to_zero/transcript?subtitle=en

"My experience tells me, that there are multiple, independent, unnecessary, and obvious mechanisms of toxicity built into these so called vaccines"[35].

— Dr. Michael Yeadon

Despite the collective 'COVID-19 vaccines' having tallied the most adverse events of all other vaccines combined in 32 years, with 1.5 million VAERS reports, the vaccines continue to find distribution to babies, children, teens, pregnant mothers,  and the public at large.

The elephant or, perhaps, more accurately the herd of elephants in the room are ignored with great and willful intent. That the deaths line up precisely with the rollout of the various COVID vaccines is undeniable. And yet it is attended by a profound and monstrous silence and/or a universe of lies. Is this not complicity in high crimes that would easily be deemed crimes against humanity?

---

[35] YEADON, M. (2024, November 11). *THE PLANNED DELIBERATE BIO WEAPON INJECTION ATTACK*. Retrieved November 12, 2024, from https://www.bitchute.com/video/DLVuieYhJD3J

An important question to ask, in light of the above, is why have government officials worldwide been given exemptions to the mandate? As Tyler Durden reports on his website *ZeroHedge*, *Members Of Congress, Staff Exempt From Biden Vaccine Mandate*[36]

> "But not included in the executive orders are mandates for members of federal employees in the legislative or judicial branches, including members of Congress, their staffers, as well as federal judges and other court employees."[37]

> "In August, a group of 19 Democrats in the House wrote a letter to the Capitol's attending physician, Dr. Brian P. Monahan, asking him to consider a vaccine requirement or a minimum of two COVID tests per week for members and

---

[36] Durden, T. (2021, September 12). *Members of Congress, Staff Exempt from Biden Vaccine Mandate*. Retrieved October 23, 2024, from https://www.zerohedge.com/covid-19/members-congress-staff-exempt-biden-vaccine-mandate

[37] Lord, J. (2021, September 10). *Members of Congress, Federal Judges, Staffers Exempt From Vaccine Mandate*. Retrieved November 1, 2024, from https://www.theepochtimes.com/us/members-of-congress-federal-judges-staffers-exempt-from-vaccine-mandate-3991881

> staff who can't show proof of vaccination. No requirement has yet been put in place."[38]

Again, ask yourself if the 'COVID-19 vaccines' were ever thought to be truly "safe and effective", why have so many government leaders and officials opted out of taking them or did not mandate them for members of congress or their governments?

Was "safe and effective" always a bridge too far, not believable, and governments and politicians knew that this phrase was not true? I imagine that there are legal consequences/ramifications given the mounting 'COVID-19 vaccine' deaths, disabilities, and the excess deaths, which tie to a baseline where 'COVID-19 vaccine' distribution had begun. This is addressed in much greater detail below. However, the questions remain, what did they know about the 'vaccines' and when did they know it?

> "You can no more make a baby in one month with nine women, than you can make a complicated biological product (a vaccine) in

---

[38] Roche, D. (2021, September 10). *Members of Congress and Their Staff Are Exempt From Biden's Vaccine Mandate*. Retrieved November 1, 2024, from https://www.newsweek.com/members-congress-staff-exempt-biden-covid-vaccine-mandate-1627859

ten months. It cannot be done. It was not done. They did something else. They created materials which essentially were injected poisons. They were not vaccines"[39].

—Dr. Michael Yeadon

Additionally, a Slovenian nurse exposed the fact that politicians and tycoons (oligarchs) received a placebo, a saline solution, 'COVID-19 vaccine'.

"A crisis has hit the eastern European country of Slovenia after a whistleblower head nurse alerted the public that politicians and other high-ranking citizens are receiving saline placebos instead of the COVID mRNA experimental vaccines"[40]

---

[39] YEADON, M. (2024, November 11). *THE PLANNED DELIBERATE BIO WEAPON INJECTION ATTACK*. Retrieved November 12, 2024, from https://www.bitchute.com/video/DLVuieYhJD3J

[40] CFT Team (2021, November 24). *Whistleblower Nurse In Slovenia Claims 30% Of COVID Vaccines Are Placebos — To Be Used On The Elite*. Retrieved November 13, 2024, from https://christiansfortruth.com/whistleblower-nurse-in-slovenia-claims-30-of-covid-vaccines-are-placebos-to-be-used-on-the-elite/

And a New Zealand whistleblower let it be known that 11,000 politicians and elites were exempted from taking the 'COVID-19 vaccine'[41].

> "An Open Government Act (FOIA) request revealed that 11,000 politicians and members of the elite had been exempted from vaccination, Michael Gray Griffin said in a conversation with doctor Paul Oosterhuis and Liz Gunn, leader of the New Zealand Loyal Party"[42].

It also appears that one of the leading proponents of 'COVID-19 vaccine' mandates, French President Emmanuel Macron was not vaccinated, nor were most members of the French parliament. Jean Lassalle, a former candidate for the presidency of France, recalled being shocked that Macron and most members of parliament did not get the jab.

---

[41] BIT CHUTE (2023, December 1). New Zealand: 11,000 COVID Vaccine Exemptions For Politicians & Elites While Coercing Vaccines. Retrieved November 13, 2024, from https://www.bitchute.com/video/kazYSO84iKA2/

[42] UNCUT-NEWS (2023, December 1). *11,000 politicians and elites received an exemption for the Covid vaccination: "This is shocking".* Retrieved November 13, 2024, from https://uncutnews.ch/11-000-politiker-und-eliten-erhielten-eine-ausnahmegenehmigung-fuer-die-covid-impfung-das-ist-erschuetternd/

> "But I did not know that Emmanuel Macron was not vaccinated. I did not know that most of the government members were not, and I did not know as many of my fellow MPs were not either. I wanted to set an example"[43].

Lassalle would undergo four heart surgeries after receiving the Johnson-Johnson 'COVID-19 vaccine'. As Mr. Lassalle commented:

> "The vaccine almost killed me…So I have had four surgeries since January 3rd of this year," he continued. "And then there is in the Ambroise Paré clinic where the surgeon trained with one who succeeded in putting the auricles in place to make them function normally. Otherwise, I would certainly be dead"[44].
>
> —Jean Lassalle

[43] Bettermann MD, E. (2022, October 17). *Macron and "most MPs are not vaccinated," reveals former French presidential candidate in shocking claim.* Retrieved November 13, 2024, from https://dreddymd.com/2022/10/17/macron-and-most-mps-not-vaccinated/

[44] Bettermann MD, E. (2022, October 17). *Macron and "most MPs are not vaccinated," reveals former French presidential candidate in shocking claim.* Retrieved November 13, 2024, from https://dreddymd.com/2022/10/17/macron-and-most-mps-not-vaccinated/

Again, this is what is known or that has come out as a result of Freedom of Information Acts (FOIA) or whistleblowers or former politicians coming forward. It is not difficult to understand that this was the rule and not the exception. If these vaccines were so "safe and effective" why did government officials across the world exempt themselves? And these are just the governments of which we are currently aware.

## HEALTHCARE & THE MASKS

I needed to include a section on masks as it was imperative to attempt to reach those who continue to wear a mask. A mask which they believe protects them but does not. In fact, wearing a mask can actually cause more damage than not wearing a mask. For instance, mask wearing can lead to—oxygen deprivation, increased CO2 uptake, hypoxia (which impairs brain development and cognition), hypercapnia, epidural abscess, etc. And when worn for even short periods of time—hours—the masks have been found to serve as an incubator for the production of bacterial and fungal colonies[45]. Masks

---

[45] Wehby, Dr., M. (2022, October 13). *Dr. Monica Wehby Debunks the Face Mask Narrative - Studies Confirm.* Retrieved December 7, 2024, from https://www.bitchute.com/video/c9KvX39vzGug

worn for extended periods of time can be very dangerous.

Further, masks do not protect you from a 'virus' that sees each hole in the fabric of the mask, in relative size, as a large, opened, screen-less window to a gnat. A smoke particle, for instance, can range in size from 2.5 to 10 micrometers[46] (μm). A 'virus' particle can range in size from 20 to 750 nanometers (nm)[47]. In terms of size the mathematical representation is as follows:

- The representation for a micrometer or micron (μm) is: 1 micron = 1/1000 mm
- The representation for a nanometer (nm) is: 1 nm = 1/1000 μm

Given the above, the difference between a micrometer and a nanometer is that a nanometer is

---

[46] Plackett, B. (n.d.). *Smoke's particle size is key to its health consequences*. https://cen.acs.org/biological-chemistry/toxicology/Smokes-particle-size-key-health/98/i39

[47] Morgridge Institute for Research (n.d.). *Virus Structure*. https://morgridge.org/community/teaching-learning/virology-immunology/factsheets/virus-structure/

1,000 times smaller than a micrometer[48], which is an order of magnitude. However, seldom, if ever do mask makers and the various public health agencies reference a 'virus" actual size, which is measured in nanometers (20-750 nm) and not micrometers (µm). The reason, of course, is obvious, it would completely invalidate the use of masks for anything other that 'wet material'—blood, saliva, and other bodily fluids—that would enter a patient's body, who is undergoing surgery. This is the reason that surgeons wear masks, not to keep out 'viral' particles.

I have seen the analogous references to a mask in relation to keeping out the 'virus', like a chain-link fence trying to keep out mosquitoes. However, given that the mesh or pores in masks can be seen by eyesight and more easily by a 5 to 10 time magnifying glass and that a 1 nanometer (nm) 'virus' requires a transmission electron microscope to view. The appropriate analogy would be like using a chain-link fence to keep out smoke.

---

[48] Khillar, S. (n.d.). *Difference Between Micron and Nanometer*. DifferenceBetween.ne. https://www.differencebetween.net/technology/difference-between-micron-and-nanometer/

Speaking of smoke, I have an experiment for those of you who are still wearing the mask or, even better, the N95 mask and brave enough to undertake this test. Have a friend or family member light a stick of incense or have a friend, who smokes, blow a stream of smoke directly into your mask. It's an experiment, after all, so this should not be considered offensive. First, you should know that, per the CDC's own infographic, a molecule of smoke is 10-microns in size, which is at the very least100 times larger than a virus. If you are able to smell the incense or your friend's cigarette smoke has easily penetrated your mask, then you should know that your mask is an abject failure at keeping out 'viral' particles. Here the logic is fairly straightforward and simple. If a smoke molecule can get through your mask, it would be, at least, 100 times easier for a 'virus' molecule to get through that same mask. I do believe that I know the outcome of this experiment—the smoke gets through, regardless of the mask being worn.

There have been a number of studies citing the lack of efficacy of wearing a mask to the potential harm and increased mortality of wearing a mask. Below are studies which speak to the phenomenon.

During 'COVID-19' Sweden kept its schools open without mask mandates, social distancing, or testing. There were 1.8 million children in the study from ages 1 to 16. As a result of their policy there were zero deaths[49] from 'COVID-19' and neither teachers nor older parents living with the children in the study were affected. There were zero deaths.

The state of Kansas with 105 counties gave each county a choice between whether to accept or to deny mask mandates. Of the 105 counties 81 chose not to accept the mask mandates, while 24 accepted the mask mandates. An observational study—"The Foegen Effect: A Mechanism by Which Face Masks Contribute to the COVID-19 Case Fatality Rate"—was published in *Medicine* February, 2002. Its author doctor Zacharias Fögen. The study was undertaken to assess the efficacy of wearing the masks in regard to 'COVID-19'. The study's finding were that:

> "The most important finding from this study is that contrary to the accepted thought that

---

[49] Walia, A. (2021, January 10). *Sweden Kept Schools Open Resulting in ZERO Deaths*. Retrieved November 6, 2024, from https://principia-scientific.com/sweden-kept-schools-open-resulting-in-zero-deaths/

> fewer people are dying because infection rates are reduced by masks, this was not the case. Results from this study strongly suggest that mask mandates actually caused about 1.5 times the number of deaths or ~50% more deaths compared to no mask mandates."[50]

The study also came to the following conclusion:

> "This study revealed that wearing a face mask might impose a great risk on individuals, which would not be mitigated by a reduction in the infection rate. The use of face masks might, therefore, be unfit if not contraindicated as an epidemiologic intervention against 'COVID-19'."[51]

Certainly the takeaway here is that not only do masks not work with regard to the 'COVID-19 virus' or any 'virus', but that they are actually more problematic

---

[50] Fögen MD, Z. (2022, February 18). *The Foegen effect A mechanism by which facemasks contribute to the COVID-19 case fatality rate*. Retrieved November 6, 2024, from https://journals.lww.com/md-journal/Fulltext/2022/02180/The_Foegen_effect__A_mechanism_by_which_facemasks.60.aspx

[51] Fögen MD, Z. (2022, February 18). *The Foegen effect A mechanism by which facemasks contribute to the COVID-19 case fatality rate*. Retrieved November 6, 2024, from https://journals.lww.com/md-journal/Fulltext/2022/02180/The_Foegen_effect__A_mechanism_by_which_facemasks.60.aspx

than wearing no mask at all and can actually lead to an increase in mortality.

Another peer reviewed observational study —"Correlation Between Mask Compliance and COVID-19 Outcomes in Europe"—also found a positive correlation between wearing mask and their, harmful effects:

> "Moreover, the moderate positive correlation between mask usage and deaths in Western Europe also suggests that the universal use of masks may have had harmful unintended consequences[52]".

Other consequences of wearing a mask are that, within minutes, pathogenic bacteria and fungi accumulate on the mask and can be cultured. This, in turn, can lead to increased risks of bacterial pneumonia, meningitis, epidural abscesses, and increased levels of CO2 (which goes above the safe level of CO2 for a mask worn for 10 minutes). As earlier pointed out, this can lead to hypoxia and

---

[52] Spira, B. (2022, April 19). *Correlation Between Mask Compliance and COVID-19 Outcomes in Europe*. Retrieved November 6, 2024, from https://www.cureus.com/articles/93826-correlation-between-mask-compliance-and-covid-19-outcomes-in-europe#!/

hypercapnia. It should be noted that hypoxia impairs brain development and cognition in children.

That children have been mandated to wear masks either reflects tremendous incompetence or it is child abuse and endangerment and is beyond evil.

For those still wearing masks in the belief that a mask can keep them safe from a 'virus' that must be seen through an electron microscope, you have been lied to and exploited. These masks have not helped you, they have, in fact, potentially harmed you. Taking them off for good is not just a symbolic gesture, though it is indeed that, but it may well save your life. Additionally, you demonstrate that you will no longer be a slave. Taking off the mask will also help you to heal physically, psychologically, and emotionally.

## SECTION THREE

### 'Earth': The Media, Society

As I wrote in an earlier book, Operation Mockingbird was a CIA disinformation program that began in the 1940s. It was used to spread propaganda throughout the US and utilized the various media—mainstream television, newspapers, and magazines, etc—to that end. In some cases, the CIA took direct control of major news outlets to spread its propaganda.

In 1975 CIA Director William Colby informed the Church Committee that the US Media was penetrated. Colby told the Church Committee that over 400 CIA agents were active in the US media in 1975 as a result of Operation Mockingbird. This, of course, was illegal. The 1948 Smith-Mundt Act forbade government agencies from directing propaganda campaigns within the United States. The Smith-Mundt Act was passed in Congress to ensure that United States citizens would not be subjected to the same type of brainwashing undertaken in World War II Germany.

Since 1975, however, the corporate-owned mainstream media has maintained a very close relationship to the CIA and other domestic spy agencies. A seasoned journalist, longtime reporter for the *Washington Post*, and one of two reporters who broke the Watergate scandal, Carl Bernstein, thought that the Church commission, in fact, covered much of the truth up. And in his 25,000 word article for Rolling Stone, *THE CIA AND THE MEDIA: How America's Most Powerful News Media Worked Hand in Glove with the Central Intelligence Agency and Why the Church Committee Covered It Up*[53], Bernstein lets that truth be known.

> "Among the chief executives who helped the CIA were William Paley of CBS, Henry Luce of Time, Arthur Sulzberger of the New York Times, Barry Bingham Sr. of the Louisville Courier-Journal, and James Copley of the Copley News Service. The leading TV networks, including ABC and NBC, and the wire services-AP, UPI, Reuters, along with Hearst Newspapers, Scripps Howard, Newsweek, the

[53] Bernstein, C. (1977, October 20). THE CIA AND THE MEDIA How Americas Most Powerful News Media Worked Hand in Glove with the Central Intelligence Agency and Why the Church Committee Covered It Up. *Rolling Stone*, (250). https://www.carlbernstein.com/the-cia-and-the-media-rolling-stone-10-20-1977

Miami Herald, and the Saturday Evening Post all had dealings with the spy agency. The CIA's most valuable associations were with the New York Times, CBS, and Time Inc".

Despite the Church Committee's findings and Bernstein's revelations, CIA office memos released under the Freedom Of Information Act (FOIA) and investigative reports by Alex Constantine and Michael Hasting (before his assassination) confirmed that CIA propaganda was, indeed, still directed at United States citizens.

In an article written by Alex Constantine entitled, "Tales from the Crypt: The Depraved Spies and Moguls of the CIA's Operation MOCKINGBIRD "[54] Constantine writes:

"Most consumers of the corporate media were - and are - unaware of the effect that the salting of public opinion has on their own beliefs. A network anchorman in time of national crisis is

---

[54] Constantine, A. (2010, February 5). *Tales from the Crypt – The Depraved Spies and Moguls of the CIA's Operation MOCKINGBIRD*. Retrieved December 7, 2024, from https://constantinereport.com/tales-from-the-crypt-the-depraved-spies-and-moguls-of-the-cias-operation-mockingbird/

> an instrument of psychological warfare in the MOCKINGBIRD media. He is a creature from the national security sectors chamber of horrors. For this reason consumers of the corporate press have reason to examine their basic beliefs about government and life in the parallel universe of these United States. In 1977, the Copely News Service admitted that it worked closely with the intelligence services—in fact, 23 employees were full-time employees of the Agency (Constantine, What Really Happened)."

Constantine goes on to state that one of the country's most revered network anchors was an intelligence asset:

> "No one ever turned a suspicious eye on Walter Cronkite, a former intelligence officer and in the immediate postwar period UPI's Moscow correspondent. Cronkite was lured to CBS by Operation MOCKINGBIRD's Phil Graham, according to Deborah Davis (Constantine, What Really Happened)."

To believe that the CIA and other intelligence agencies have ceased their propaganda campaigns directed at US citizens and have relinquished their control of the media, would be foolish in the extreme. What we witness today is the complete and absolute capture of mainstream media in all of its varied forms as well as deep connections and agents in the alternative media as well. The recent 'COVID-19 pandemic' puts paid to that.

When Erwin Knoll (July 17,1931 – November 2, 1994), Editor of the *Progressive*, showed up on the *MacNeil Lehrer Newshour* in the early 1990's it would represent the *Newshour's* swan-song, its too little, too late attempt at balance. Balance so as not to so completely toe the accepted 'company' line. Shortly before he died, Erwin Knoll, perhaps, the last un-captured media editor, embarrassed the usual suspects of the mainstream media one night. On that night as the usual suspects feted and fetished war and its 'gloriously' destructive, 'pretty' weapons, Erwin reminded them that there were innocent people being slaughtered by those very same 'pretty' weapons. It was a deer in the headlights moment for the usual suspects, as quiet fell for the briefest of instants. That statement by Erwin had so succinctly said it all, summed it up across the entirety of the mainstream media—you are but mouthpieces for war.

Below is a pictograph of media consolidation prior to the latest rounds of consolidation which find not six but five companies controlling the assets that were once held by 50 media companies in 1983. Those companies are (1) GE (2) NEWS-CORP (3) DISNEY (4) TIME WARNER and (5) NATIONAL AMUSEMENTS (formerly Paramount Global, which had controlled both Viacom and CBS).

There were a great many then opposed to the unending media concentration, as they believed it would place undue power and control in the hands of a minute few. This would give them the power to control the narrative of events, positively, in its best interest and, negatively, with regard to those events that challenged its interest. And what we witness as I write this book is exactly that.

The practice of shunning or banning or castigating the voices of those who oppose the status quo policies of—endless war, censorship, the stripping away of informed consent, vaccine mandates, etc—has, perhaps, never been more all encompassing. The East German Stasi, the Soviets, the era of

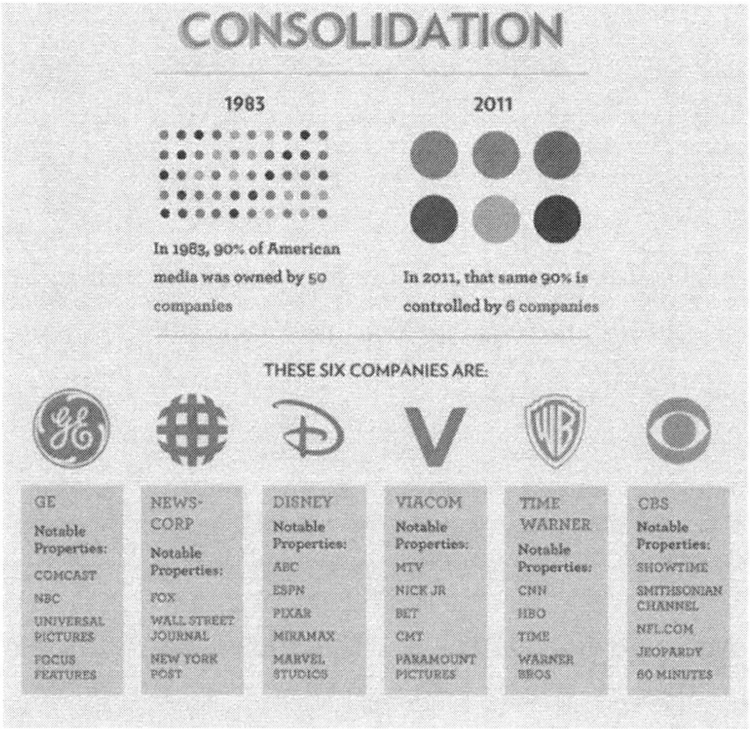


McCarthyism in this respect, are all found wanting in relation to the totalitarianism now being casually implemented in the 'democratic' West. This while its well-funded divide and conquer regimes—'Woke', 'Black Lives Matter', 'Antifa', etc.—wreak havoc on any chance of a united front. This is, of course, their intention as all of the above listed regimes are funded by billionaires. Could it not be more clear?

Meanwhile the silence is, truly, deafening on those policies that would enrich, better the lives of the balance of the population, the 99%. Policies such as single-payer healthcare[55], a living wage, affordable housing, reimbursed childcare, a well maintained public commons, greatly decreased war spending, etc. On these topics, the tactic is simply to ignore all who would champion such policies and deny them access to any position of political/governmental or a media body that would give them voice.

Though the most important aspect of such overwhelming control is setting the narrative and its continuous propagation, in 'lockstep', across media and other connected assets. This was demonstrated in the 'COVID-19 pandemic' wherein the mainstream media, the 'alternative media', governments, academia, corporatocracy, private and public 'healthcare', pharmaceutical companies, and their 'regulatory' agencies, etc. all walked, preached, argued, cajoled in lockstep. This mass cult-programming on a scale the likes of which Joseph Goebbels would have been proud. For as Goebbels

[55] Though in the current atmosphere of 'COVID-19' it could well have been a disadvantage. Knowledge gained will stop that.

knew, any shred of truth that penetrates this echo chamber could well be fatal.

> "If you tell a lie big enough and keep repeating it, people will eventually come to believe it. The lie can be maintained only for such time as the State can shield the people from the political, economic and/or military consequences of the lie. It thus becomes vitally important for the State to use all of its powers to repress dissent, for the truth is the mortal enemy of the lie, and thus by extension, the truth is the greatest enemy of the State"
>
> —Joseph Goebbels, Nazi Party Reich Minister of Propaganda

Understand, the only parallels for this, again, are Nazi Germany's Third Reich, the Soviet Union, East Germany's Stasi, and US McCarthyism, though they all pale in comparison.

Thus the immediate censoring, removal of media, de-platforming, shadow banning, etc. was of critical importance for the lie to be maintained. Further, an army of 'fact checker's was necessary to take down any and all whistleblowers, regarding 'COVID-19', many who would have been believed. These were not your average 'conspiracy theorists' (who more often than not tend to see truth well before others), these were whistleblowers, who had spent their entire adult, professional lives in the pharmaceutical industry or as researchers, doctors, professors of genetics, biology, microbiology, etc. They were the true professionals of this 'COVID-19 pandemic'. And this army of 'fact checkers', who had not a fraction of the breadth or the knowledge or the experience were unleashed upon them with a kind of ignorant vitriol that was astonishing. The 'fact checkers' were, in turn, the starkest of amateurs, at best.

There are important ways of seeing through the 'fact checkers'. For instance, who pays them, who do they work for, and do they ever 'fact check' the establishment's side of things? For the great many who have never thought of doing this, now may be the time. I have heard it said that the 'fact checkers' emerged as the truth began to shine through. I do not doubt the accuracy of this statement for a single moment.

There are several key points to understand with regard to the media. The first of which is that telling the truth is not a concern of the media and its spokespeople/actors, who we call news people. There are far too many compilations of news people saying, in lockstep, the exact same thing. I'm certain that you've seen them. If not you may wish to pull one of the videos up, assuming that they have not all been scrubbed or banned. Who do you think is handing them their scripts?

Certainly the mainstream news media have become no more than an appendage of government and would more accurately be referred to as the Federal News Media Association (FNMA). It would be an understatement to say that what issues forth from the mainstream media is what government, the intelligence agencies, big business, etc. tell it to say. Anyone in this day and age who is still 'informed' by the mainstream media and its perpetual big lie is detached, entirely, from 'reality' itself. The mainstream media, FNMA, is the antithesis of the truth.

Over a decade ago, when I wrote my first book, I used the internet as both a source of information and a guide to books that would further help me in that research. It was a very useful tool and, more often than not, it provided me with the information that I needed. It was a good experience.

Today, as I seek to do even the most minimal research on a given individual and certainly if that individual has not surrendered to the mainstream narrative, most often they are not found. Instead what comes, though I've typed in a specific name with quotes about it, are the 'fact checkers'. I see blistering critiques, ad hominem attacks, that seek to discredit the searched for person, before that person ever shows up! Sometimes if you look deeply into the search results you may find an alternative view of the mainstream's dictum, but this has grown increasingly rare. There could be no clearer case of Goebbels' above quote that "the truth is the greatest enemy of state". This is a crystal clear indication of his statement.

As an example, when I searched for former Pfizer Executive Dr. Michael Yeadon[56], "an experienced life

---

[56] UK Column (2025, January 13). *Licence to Kill: Drugs with Consequences — With Dr Mike Yeadon*. Retrieved January 14, 2025, from https://www.ukcolumn.org/video/licence-to-kill-drugs-with-consequences-with-dr-mike-yeadon

sciences R&D professional, with 32 years in commercial R&D"[57], I got 'fact checkers' Snopes[58], Reuters[59], Politifact[60] Full Fact, Yahoo, etc. Here was a former Pfizer executive and insider aware not only of Pfizer's structure, policies, etc. but who had developed drugs while in their employ for the some part of his 32 years in pharma.

To read or to see any videos by Dr. Yeadon is to get insight into why he is so very dangerous. His experience and inside information and knowledge of drug discovery is invaluable to destroying the 'COVID-19' narrative. It has been said that once a lie has established itself via repetitivity, it is nearly

---

[57] Yeadon, Dr., M. (2022, April 10). *The Covid Lies*. Retrieved November 1, 2024, from https://mikeyeadon.com/covid-lies

[58] Did Michael Yeadon Say COVID-19 Vaccine Will Kill Recipients Within 2 Years?, Madison Dapcevich: https://www.snopes.com/fact-check/michael-yeadon-vaccine-death/

[59] The ex-Pfizer scientist who became an anti-vax hero, Reuters: https://www.reuters.com/investigates/special-report/health-coronavirus-vaccines-skeptic/

[60] "Head of Pfizer research: Covid vaccine is female sterilization." Ciara O'Rourke, Politifact: https://www.politifact.com/factchecks/2020/dec/10/blog-posting/no-pfizers-head-research-didnt-say-covid-19-vaccin/

impossible for those exposed to the lie to see the truth. This is why a battery of 'fact checkers' must come first. They must establish the 'big lie' well before any shred of truth outs.

I have experienced this as I have tried to provide information to friends stuck in the narrative, so that they might understand from someone in the industry, a whistleblower. I have also sent information on Pfizer's own internal documents that Pfizer and the FDA tried to keep concealed for 75 years and the devastating truth behind them[61 62]. Often, the very first thing done or said, is "I can come up with sources that disprove what you've sent me." This is even before having read or looked deeply into the information or the person or persons that I have sent them. This is a reflex action, of course, which the 'first lie' has helped to program, it is a reactionary response. Further, it is the response of an individual, who has been mass cult-programmed or

---

[61] Wolf Dr , N. (2022, May 29). Dear Friends, Sorry to Announce a Genocide. Retrieved October 29, 2024, from https://naomiwolf.substack.com/p/dear-friends-sorry-to-announce-a?s=r

[62] Wolf, N., & Kelly, A. (2024). The Pfizer Papers: Pfizer's Crimes Against Humanity. War Room Books.

brainwashed. The idea of simply taking the time to read and think about the information, free of pre-judging it, is simply out of the question. And I know both personally and through the stories of friends, that this is so and has resulted in broken friendships, threats of broken friendships, and of estranged families, and loved ones.

"Well, isn't their truth, the real truth?" Is it, when a respiratory flu 'virus' can result in myocarditis, pericarditis, Sudden Adult Death Syndrome (SADS), menstrual dysregulation, MS, Guillain Barre, Bell's Palsy, etc.? Or when a "safe and effective" 'vaccine' has 1.5 million adverse events that have been reported on the Government's own Vaccine Adverse Events Reporting System (VAERS)? This number, 1.5, million, again represents more adverse events than all the vaccines combined over the past 32 years! Is their truth of "safe and effective" a truth at all? I do repeat this fact quite often, but it is very important.

What flu has ever caused any of the above? No flu. What has, in fact, historically caused many or most of the adverse conditions, inclusive of death, listed above? Prescription medicines and vaccines[63]. This fact the book *Dissolving Illusions: Disease, Vaccines, and The Forgotten History* by authors Suzanne Humphries, MD and Roman Bystrianyk has so meticulously documented. The cornerstone of the status quo's arguments have crumbled to dust. The truth is that the mainstream's arguments have never stood on firm ground. Have the 'fact checkers' checked this? They have not.

In another interesting twist, several African presidents and a Haitian president who opposed 'COVID-19 vaccines' died and were soon thereafter replaced by a president, who favored the 'vaccination'.

> "The leaders of three different countries died after having stopped the distribution of the experimental Covid-19 jabs. All three countries took the decision to distribute the vaccines to

[63] Bystrianyk, R., & Humphries MD, S. (2013). *Dissolving Illusions: Disease, Vaccines, and The Forgotten History* (1st ed., p. 504). CreateSpace Independent Publishing Platform. https://www.amazon.com/Dissolving-Illusions-Disease-Vaccines-Forgotten/dp/1480216895

> their citizens only after their leaders passed away."[64]

Happenstance? Cruel irony? The five leaders were from Burundi, Swaziland, Tanzania, Ivory Coast, and Haiti. If you are reading this book, it is highly probable that you are aware of these close-together deaths that held a common denominator—opposition to 'COVID-19 vaccines'. The 'fact checkers' would like you to believe that only one was assassinated because gunmen came for him directly. The others, the 'fact checkers' would lead you to believe, all died of natural causes in a considerably tight time period. The other common denominator—'COVID-19 vaccine' refusal—is completely overlooked. Further, that they were all replaced by pro-vaccine distribution presidents, is neither here nor there for the 'fact checker'. Don't investigations begin with trying to establish a common denominator among victims, who in this case were

---

[64] Rucker, J. (2021, August 1). *Five Presidents Who Opposed Covid Vaccines Have Conveniently Died, Been Replaced by Pro-Vaxxers*. Retrieved November 1, 2024, from https://newsrescue.com/five-presidents-who-opposed-covid-vaccines-have-conveniently-died-been-replaced-by-pro-vaxxers/

all presidents of a Haitian and of African countries, who opposed 'COVID-19'?

A film script that laid out the above scenario would be deemed "on the nose"—something with indelicate or awkward directness; lacking subtlety or nuance[65]. That is "it's way too obvious" and you'd be asked to rewrite it. Yet 'fact checkers' are completely oblivious.

To restate, five presidents who are against the distribution of 'COVID-19 vaccines' in their countries are dead. One is very obviously assassinated and the other four 'all died suddenly', in a rather tight time period. They are all replaced by pro-'COVID-19 vaccine' distribution presidents. Nothing to see here folks but a coincidence repeated four times. Move on.

Believing a 'fact checkers', who, by the way, don't 'fact check' government claims (a much easier job, as there are volumes of evidence against their claims), is like buying the same public bridge over and over

---

[65] For Farlex Dictionary of Idioms:
on the nose. (n.d.) Farlex Dictionary of Idioms. (2015). Retrieved November 2 2024 from https://idioms.thefreedictionary.com/on+the+nose

again, and thinking that one of these times, you'll actually own it. Perhaps fact deniers would be a more appropriate label.

Mainstream media has long been broken and in this broken state what remains is bought and paid for. It is bought and paid for by those who wish to push a narrative or propaganda, if you will, that is very often, if not always at odds with what the 'people' want. And, of course, they have to lie, because if they told the truth, folks simply wouldn't buy it.  For instance:

"Hey, listen up. We're going to gin-up some wars in the Middle East cause there's lots of oil there and it gives us control over it and both a look-see and a blocking position against everybody else. And we'd be helping out our good ole buddy there too. And, yes, your sons and some daughters are going to die over there or they'll be seriously injured, but not my sons and daughters and that's good. And we'll get nice fat brides/kickbacks, and military spending will increase and all, and you'll become poorer  and less safe all the time ".

This could have been said by any number of presidents, if any of them were to have been honest. Instead you got "9/11", "WMD", "Saddam hearts Osama", "Killing his own people", "A mushroom cloud," etc. Question, when did the government stop lying to you and when did the media stop parroting those lies?

The other side of the media coin of censorship and suppression of information is social media. Yes, social media—Facebook, YouTube, Instagram, LinkedIn, etc.—that censors, removes 'offensive' content, de-platforms, shadow bans, and 'fact checks'. Apparently, they don't believe that its users are intelligent enough to make their own informed decisions regarding material that is posted to their sites. Or, they do believe that its users are intelligent enough and they do not wish to bring scrutiny to issues that will not stand up under closer examination. Either way, it's bad for all the social media companies who indulge in censorship and 'fact checking' and it's really not a good thing for those using social media (see Patronizing). You are here.

## THE SOCIETY

It has been said that the measure of a good society is how that society treats its most vulnerable, the overall health of the society, how it looks after its commons—public, shared spaces—the society's general fellowship, and how wealth is distributed.

The most vulnerable in any given society are its children. Then there are those who are most aged, the sick and infirmed—physically, mentally, psychologically—and the destitute.

There are 11 million children in poverty in the US, nearly 1 in 7[66]. And of these children 7 to 11 million go underfed and hungry with the rising cost of food a major factor among a host of others (see Inflation via War). The US, one of 37 countries in the Organization for Economic Cooperation and Development (OECD), ranks last in regard to child

---

[66] Haider, A. (2021, January 21). *The Basic Facts About Children in Poverty*. Retrieved January 3, 2024, from https://www.americanprogress.org/article/basic-facts-children-poverty/

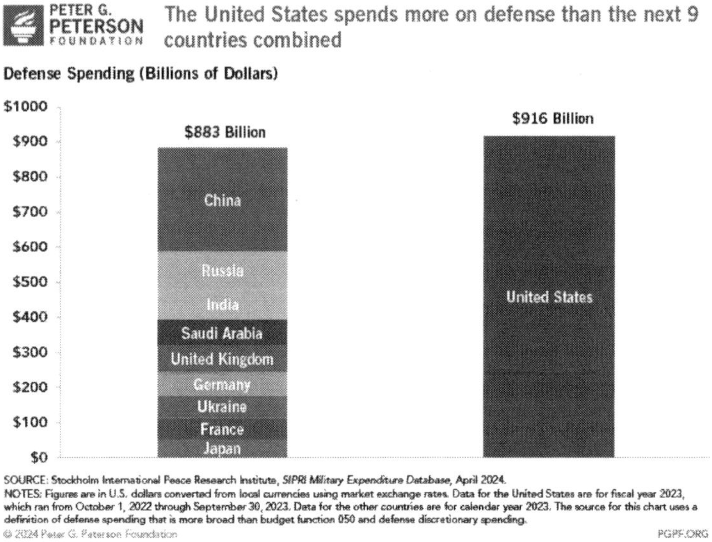


poverty[67] or the worst of all others. This is happening in the world's wealthiest country and it is an appalling inversion.

No doubt, a major reason for this over the decades has been war as an inflationary/wealth concentrating engine, the ongoing demonization and deconstruction of the social safety net—medicaid, social security, unemployment insurance, disability insurance, etc. These programs of social uplift have been derisively referred to as welfare or more

---

[67] Organization for Economic Cooperation and Development, "Poverty rate," available at https://data.oecd.org/inequality/poverty-rate.htm (last accessed January 2021).

appropriately welfare for the people. And even in its past and current form these programs are but a shadow of what they should be. And, of course, there were the campaigns that targeted the poor, the welfare mother's with an almost relentless and dualistic zeal—they are other.

This while both corporate welfare and the military industrial complex's welfare has grown to unprecedented levels. The irony, of course, is that those who had demonized welfare for the people have wholeheartedly supported welfare for corporations and the military. For example, the US military spent $916 billion on national defense in 2023, which was more than the next nine[68] countries combined.

One Mississippi Senator, Roger Wicker, even sought help from the Heritage Foundation to raise the defense budget to $1.4 trillion dollars for 2024, a

---

[68] Peter G. Peterson Foundation (2024, April 22). *The United States Spends More on Defense than the Next 9 Countries Combined*. Retrieved November 3, 2024, from https://www.pgpf.org/blog/2024/04/the-united-states-spends-more-on-defense-than-the-next-9-countries-combined

nearly 50% increase from 2023[69]. Senator Wicker's state, Mississippi, interestingly, is the third poorest state in the nation with an 18% poverty rate[70]. Got social welfare?

Given the formidable disparity and irony between social spending and military spending, there is not a modicum of irony or shame or remorse, from those, who in lockstep, denigrated social welfare recipients. In truth, both the corporate and the military industrial complex have been feted by the government, mainstream media, academia, etc., which spend nearly a trillion dollars each year. And yet, 11 million of the country's children, its most vulnerable population, live in poverty, with food insecurity rising almost daily.

In terms of those over 65 years of age, who live in poverty, the US has the distinction of being number

---

[69] Harris, B. (2024, March 7). *A nearly $1 trillion defense budget faces headwinds at home and abroad*. Retrieved November 3, 2024, from https://www.defensenews.com/congress/2024/03/07/a-nearly-1-trillion-defense-budget-faces-headwinds-at-home-and-abroad/

[70] The Friends Committee on National Legislation (2024, September 17). *Top 10 Poorest States in the US* Retrieved November 3, 2024, from https://www.fcnl.org/updates/2024-09/top-10-poorest-states-us

three at 21.5%, behind Switzerland 23.4% and Australia 33.4%[71].

> "More than 17 million older adults age 65+ are economically insecure, with incomes below 200% of the federal poverty level."[72]

Further, with rising inflation and a federal poverty level of $15,060 for 2024, even those at 200% of the federal poverty level are struggling. And future prospects are not encouraging. Other key measures regarding those 65+ years old[73]:

- About 6 to 8 million adults ages 65 and older were living in poverty in 2022, depending on the measure used to assess poverty.

---

[71] Ghilarducci, T. (2018, March 2). *America's Unusual High Rates Of Old-Age Poverty And Old-Age Work*. Retrieved November 3, 2024, from https://www.forbes.com/sites/teresaghilarducci/2018/03/02/americas-unusual-high-rates-of-old-age-poverty-and-old-age-work/

[72] National Council on Aging, Inc. (2024, June 1). *Get the Facts on Economic Security for Seniors*. Retrieved November 4, 2024, from https://www.ncoa.org/article/get-the-facts-on-economic-security-for-seniors/

[73] Ochieng, N., Cubanski, J., & Neuman, T. (2024, May 21). *How Many Older Adults Live in Poverty?* Retrieved November 4, 2024, from https://www.healthcare.gov/glossary/federal-poverty-level-fpl/

- Among adults ages 65 and older, the poverty rate was higher among people ages 80 and older, women, people of color, and people in relatively poor health under both the official and supplemental poverty measures.
- The share of people ages 65 and older with incomes below the official poverty measure varied by state, ranging from 4.5% in Wisconsin to 20.3% in the District of Columbia (and from 4.2% in Iowa to 22.0% in the District of Columbia based on the Supplemental Poverty Measure).
- Between 2013 and 2022, the poverty rate among older adults remained relatively stable based on the official poverty measure, around 10%.

One imagines the many bellwethers of a given society's resilience, health or alternatively its maladies would be that society's mental health. In other words, how it copes with or does not cope with decline, disintegration, a loss of societal cohesion, the catastrophic inversion of a country's various systems. And with all of the above maladies raging simultaneously there should be little wonder of the proliferation of mental health issues and what has been described as a mental health crisis in the US.

The report "The Current State of Mental Health"[74] in America states very clearly the crisis which increasingly affects the country. In 2019, prior to the onset of the 'pandemic' there were 50 million or 1 in 5 Americans who were suffering from mental illness. What was an alarming number of people suffering from mental illness has increased since the 'pandemic', as a direct result, the report states, of "illness, job loss, isolation, rising medical costs, and financial insecurity."

The crisis of mental illness affects almost literally every aspect of society, which as the report states has a ripple effect. Some of the other key points in the report:

- Mental health disorders drive Americans to emergency room visits more than any other cause outside of childbirth.
- 12% of all emergency room visits are a result of mental health disorders.

---

[74] Plan Street (2022, April 6). *The Current State of Mental Health in America*. Retrieved November 4, 2024, from https://www.planstreetinc.com/the-current-state-of-mental-health-in-america/

- It is estimated that $193 billion in the United States economy is lost in earnings each year due to mental illness.
- 70% of American minors in the juvenile justice system are struggling with a mental health disorder.
- Over a third of US adults incarcerated have been diagnosed with a mental illness.
- Depression is the overall leading cause of disability in the United States.
- 15% of United States veterans experienced mental illness in the year 2019 alone.
- 55% of the 50,000 veterans that are incarcerated report mental health problems.
- 70% of American youth in the juvenile justice system have been diagnosed with a mental illness.
- 42% of workers whose jobs were deemed "essential" during the pandemic reported symptoms of anxiety and depression versus 30% of other Americans.
- 22% of essential workers entertained suicidal thoughts versus 8% of the general American population during the pandemic.

The addictions which stem from the crisis of mental illness are many. They range from addiction to social media, to drugs, to smoking, drinking, sex, technology (smart phones, computers, video games, internet), gambling, shopping, food, work, pornography, to even exercise[75].

Despite the overall proliferation of addictions due to mental health issues, some addictions—social media—have come into being, via their purposed design, which facilitates "repeat, compulsive use" and leads to mental illness.

> "The platforms [social media] encourage repeat, compulsive use, and now we know from psychology that only these kind of emotions aggression, envy, hatred, only these kind of emotions encourage repeated use"
>
> —Professor Sam Vaknin

> "Facebook, Twitter, all these networks; are surfing the wave. They know it's a dangerous wave, they know people are drowning. They read all the statistics, the increase in suicide rate, depression, anxiety, the know absolutely everything. They have designed maliciously, malevolently, and possibly criminally. They have designed the algorithms and networks

---

[75] Wakim M.D., D. R. (n.d.). *20 Types of Addiction: Physical and Behavioral*. White Light Behavioral Health. https://whitelightbh.com/resources/addiction-types/

exactly to cater to human pathology in (SP) its most extreme form."

—Professor Sam Vaknin

Some of the statistic regarding the effects of social media on the population and on its more vulnerable segment—our children— are as follows:

- Teens prefer to interact with other teens exclusively via social media, the number of face to face interactions dropped 70%...in 10 years.[76]
- Teenage dating has dropped 63%
- [Social media] has increased suicide by 31% among teens

And when utilized with a 'smartphone' social media's influence can become even more devastating. In 2022 48.7 million "Americans experienced a substance use disorder in the past year"[77]. In one category alone, on the behavioral side, nearly 97% or 330.8 million

---

[76] Sam Vaknin: True toxicity of Social Media

[77] Sugue, M., & Coy, A. (n.d.). 2024 Addiction Statistics: Accurate Data on Substance Abuse in the US. Addiction Group. https://www.addictiongroup.org/resources/addiction-statistics/

Americans own a smartphone and 57% or 188.5 million of those Americans consider themselves smartphone addicts, who check their phones 144 times per day. Other statistics on smartphone addiction:

- Three in four admit to feeling uncomfortable without their phones.
- One in six sleep with their phones at night.
- Almost half (47%) say that they panic when their battery drops below 20%.
- Roughly half of teens ages 13 to 27 are worried that they spend too much time on their phones.[78]

In one behavioral category alone—smartphone addiction—the numbers representing addiction find 237 million Americans suffering some form of addiction with the balance of behavioral addictions—gambling, shopping, food, work, social media, pornography, exercise, video games, internet—uncounted. The current US population numbers

---

[78] Bazen, A., & Schmitt, K. (n.d.). *Cell phone statistics 2024*. https://www.consumeraffairs.com/cell_phones/cell-phone-statistics.html

337,286,500[79] and smartphone addiction, alone at 237 million, speaks to a country in which 70% of its citizens, at the very least, suffer from addiction. Given these numbers it is entirely possible, highly probable that there is cross addiction, which may dramatically affect the percentages upward.

'Smartphone' addiction alone may be a telling bellwether of profound societal collapse and disintegration. This as young 'smartphone' users, those born and raised in the 'smartphone' era, experience social isolation in the midst of others via "phubbing"[80]—attending to one's phone when in the presence of others. Some of the issues associated with excessive smartphone use are as follows:

- Depression
- Anxiety
- Remorse

---

79 US Census Bureau (n.d.). Measuring America's People, Places, and Economy (Oct. 19, 2024). https://www.census.gov/

80 Chotpitayasunondh V, Douglas KM. How "phubbing" becomes the norm: The antecedents and consequences of snubbing via smartphone. Comput Human Behav 2016;63:9–18. 10.1016/j.chb.2016.05.018: https://www.sciencedirect.com/science/article/pii/S0747563216303454?via%3Dihub

- Psychological distress
- Diminished academic performance
- Insomnia[81]

Other issues associated with severe smartphone use were suicidal ideation, suicide attempts[82], and low emotional stability[83].

As your children and, perhaps, even you fade into your smartphones, forever praying to the small rectangular device, held in a bowed reverence, you suffer a most profound addiction. It is a technological addiction, perhaps, more powerful, more psychologically impactful than any other technological device extant. And it suffers no interference from anyone—cherished loved ones,

---

[81] Pera, A. (n.d.). The Psychology of Addictive Smartphone Behavior in Young Adults: Problematic Use, Social Anxiety, and Depressive Stress. https://www.frontiersin.org/journals/psychiatry/articles/10.3389/fpsyt.2020.573473/full

[82] Abi-Jaoude E, Naylor KT, Pignatiello A. Smartphones, social media use and youth mental health. CMAJ. 2020 Feb 10;192(6):E136-E141. doi: 10.1503/cmaj.190434. PMID: 32041697; PMCID: PMC7012622.

[83] Shoukat S. Cell phone addiction and psychological and physiological health in adolescents. EXCLI J. 2019 Feb 4;18:47-50. PMID: 30956638; PMCID: PMC6449671.

family, children, parents, etc. I have seen very young children seated as if alone on crowded buses, subways in populous, unsafe cities. Their parent(s) were seemingly unaware of them, as they bowed over their 'smartphone'. Or couples seated together at tables having dinner, yet completely oblivious to their dinner mate and entranced by their 'smartphone'. And 'smartphones' are everywhere, these days, even in the gyms, that I work out in.

Suffice to say, that given the statistics, the consequences of just one addiction—social media—across two devices—computers, smartphones—are truly staggering. Should the numbers and or crossover of the remaining forms of addiction be taken into account, to say that the US was awash in mental illness and addiction would not be an understatement. It would be closer to fact.

'EARTH'

This is 'Earth'. You live on a planet that is constantly at war, war that has taken the lives of over 200 million beings the past century alone. War that drives the economy to ruination and disintegration, and that drives the environment to inhabitability and desolation (nuclear waste, radiation, depleted uranium). Few are aware that war is purposed to impoverish and to concentrate wealth and also to destroy. War is inflationary.

Further, the society in which you currently live is splintering into tens, if not a hundred pieces—he, she, they, them, straight, LGBTQIA+, white, black, red, blue, green, catholic, protestant, muslim, jewish, buddhist, rich, poor, vanishing middle-class, etc.—and each splinter is being weaponized against the other. Ask yourself, who benefits from the structured fractionalization of the populace? Who stands to gain? Who stands to lose? And who is easy pickings, thereafter, as divided we fall?

This then is duality and the moment you choose a given splinter or several, as opposed to the whole, you have already lost. Yet few can see this and most are not even remotely aware that this is the antithesis of life, of unconditional love, of peace, wisdom, of truth. And thus the balance of society has been inverted and mis-educated? Mis-educated?

> "Several of our Young People were formerly brought up at the Colleges of the Northern

Provinces; they were instructed in all your Sciences; but when they came back to us they were bad Runners, ignorant of every means of living in the Woods, unable to bear either Cold or Hunger, knew neither how to build a Cabin, take a Deer, or kill an Enemy, spoke our Language imperfectly; were therefore neither fit for Hunters, Warriors, or Counsellors; they were totally good for nothing."

—A Chief of the Six Nations (1783)[84]

The above quote could not more accurately reflect where education has placed us here in these United States and especially those who attend to their 'educations' today.

The schools do not educate. A minimum of 12 years of education, in this day and age, does not prepare one for 'life'. It prepares one to be a cog in the system, undervalued, underpaid, unemployed, forced to the margins of society. Sixteen years, inclusive of a college degree, provides little more than the twelve years with a burden of unmanageable debt, should

---

[84] Remarks concerning the Savages of North America, [before 7 January 1784], Library of Congress, Benjamin Franklin: https://founders.archives.gov/documents/Franklin/01-41-02-0280#BNFN-01-41-02-0280-fn-0018

one have needed to take out loans. And advanced 'education', perhaps better labeled indoctrination, requires no more than the regurgitation of 'established' information, dogma. Information that is to be rewritten in tests, re-spoken in oral tests, revalidated in order to receive a degree, any degree, advanced or otherwise. Failure to properly regurgitate and you will fail. The system of education in this society does not educate, does not prepare one for 'life', does not teach one to critically think or to question. It teaches those in its 'care' to obey and to follow its dogma, right or wrong.

What was once dispensed to the indigenous peoples of this continent, is now being dispensed to you. Each subsequent generation is less able to chart its own 'life' and to live independently from their parents. Each generation is less able to purchase a home, to gain lifelong, well paying employment that allows them to provide for their children, and to gain some measure of leisure. One result is an inversion, a devolution with homelessness growing dramatically across the entire country, disintegrated families, one-parent families, zero-parent families—orphans, etc.

Intellectuals and scholars have become the antithesis of intellectuals and scholars as they are the great cowed, the frightened, the easily led and easily paid off, part of the problem. In truth, they or most have long ago abandoned integrity, common sense, and wisdom (see 'COVID-19'). They can be quite easily purchased or threatened with the loss of their careers, or the loss of their lives.

> "The reason that you cannot trust doctors any longer is because doctors are compromised. They are controlled. Their actions are controlled by a group—The Medical Council—for their income."
>
> —Dr. Sam Bailey, *The Final Pandemic*

The public health system does not cure or heal, nor provide for societal health. It is not proactive, it is reactive, its tools are petroleum inspired drugs, surgery, and chemical 'therapy', this is all it knows. It is called allopathic medicine and it was the third leading cause of death in this society until recently. However, given the past three years—the COVID-19 years—there is the high probability that it has taken over the number one spot, on the top ten causes of death. Perhaps this is why Iatrogenesis is no longer on this list of top causes of death, but 'COVID-19', the flu, with a 99.8% recovery rate has somehow made the list. Inversion.

The various public law enforcement agencies, in general (there may still be exceptions), do not 'serve and protect.' They instead intimidate, threaten, beat, coerce, falsely imprison, and kill those, who are ostensibly under its 'protection.' This as they become, step by step, paramilitaries at the behest of the cabal-below, who are behind the government frontmen and women. What they do not understand is that it is only a matter of time and that they too will be on the receiving end of the cabal-below (see AI).

The legal system is the antithesis of itself. It no longer prosecutes the powerful, whether they are frontmen and women or part of the cabal or, literally, responsible for an ongoing fraud which entails the deaths of hundreds, thousands, and millions of people across the US, a democide. Yet they will not move on the culprits even with evidence—tens of thousands of pages—from the culprits themselves. Evidence which speaks with crystal clarity to the vast crimes and crimes against humanity with great detail.

The legal system has become a for hire industry, in general, that does not protect those who cannot afford to be protected.

Greed is the society's newest religion as its other 'religions' lie desiccated, hollow, mute, spiritless in the face of an ongoing democide. The society fetishes wealth, the insanely wealthy, those who pose as populist (and are yet billionaires), and hangs on to their every lie. The history of the greed-mongers is inconsequential to society, though a rock-solid forecast of what can be expected. And when the expected comes and the lies proven, society ignores, forgets or is bereft of the capacity to critically think via an 'education' that has made it so.

In the end, you have been lied to by those who you trusted, believed good people, friends, perhaps, even 'salt of the Earth'. The lies so thick and continuous as to constitute a worldwide campaign of cult-programming, and indoctrination on a level that no cult could dare match. It has all led to fraud of catastrophic proportions (see 'COVID-19'). This fraud has enabled an ongoing, worldwide democide, whose numbers reach into the tens of millions and may soon reach into the hundreds of millions. The smoking guns of this, in the US alone, are many—athletes dropping dead, multitudinous cases of 'cause of death unknown', Sudden Adult Death Syndrome (SADS), your friends, family, and loved ones, and your children dying all around you. And you have been led to believe that a flu is responsible, when it is actually the supposed 'cure', the 'COVID-19 vaccine' that is demonstrably responsible for the ongoing democide. It is a democide that has been perpetrated against you by governments the world over, by public and private healthcare organizations, and thus every doctor, nurse, pharmacist, who continues, to this day, to administer the biotoxins posing as 'vaccines'. They have all lied to you and at this writing are engaged, still, in democide, a crime against 'humanity'.

Why are all of the above systems antithetical to life as is perceived? Because they all serve a very well-defined purpose. It is a purpose that has been kept from you for a very long time. It is a purpose that few will scarce believe.

And one last but tremendously important question, a series of questions really. When do fires fail to burn down very flammable trees immediately beside homes that have, literally, burned to the ground? When do these same fires melt engine blocks and car windows and aluminum tires, but then fail to burn down very flammable trees immediately beside or above the burned out cars or even to burn the grass around them (https://www.youtube.com/watch?v=H93Nxf6l53I)?[85] Time to wake up.

Given all of the above, which together paint a rather monstrous picture of a war-ridden, destructive, greed-mongering, democidal, and hateful society, where do you truly think that you are? Is the 'Earth' upon which you 'live' closer to Infinite Reality, Heaven or closer to Hell? The answer to this question will be very instructive going forward.

---

[85] https://www.youtube.com/watch?v=H93Nxf6l53I

# CHAPTER THREE

## SECTION ONE

### EARTH SIMULATION: YOU ARE HERE

> "This is your last chance. After this, there is no turning back. You take the blue pill – the story ends, you wake up in your bed and believe whatever you want to believe. You take the red pill – you stay in Wonderland, and I show you how deep the rabbit hole goes. Remember, all I'm offering is the truth – nothing more."
>
> —Morpheus, *The Matrix*

The 'Earth' is part of a dimensional simulation, along with everything else which you have taken as reality. The air, water, the sun, the moon, the stars, etc. are no more than holograms that comprise the simulation. The simulation is a dream fed into your Infinite Spiritual consciousness, in the selfsame way that a visor and assorted kit provide a simulated experience for its wearer. Yet it is far more complex than any currently produced simulated experience. Its pixels are what we have referred to as subatomic matter—electrons, neutrons, protons, quarks, etc.

This is the reason that subatomic matter—the 'matter' of which they are composed—is never there and can never be found. Regardless of how deeply scientists search, subatomic matter's 'physical' existence is elusive. And the fundamental reason for this, is that they are but the 'pixels' of the hologram, the computer code beneath the holographic matrix and are only numbers. This same realization is also found at the level of DNA, where the symbols or codes—A, C, G, T—can be represented by the binary numbers 0 and 1 (A,C=0; G,T=1). In this respect, our 'genetic code' is computer code.

Dr. Rich Terrile is a scientist, astronomer, and the Director of the Center for Evolutionary Computation and Automated Design at NASA's Jet Propulsion Laboratory. He is also the Voyager scientist, who discovered several moons of Saturn, Uranus, and Neptune[86]. Dr Terrile is a proponent of the simulation hypothesis—the idea that our reality is a computer-generated virtual reality created by

---

[86] Blunck, Jürgen (2009-07-01). *Solar System Moons: Discovery and Mythology*. Springer. pp. 59, 94. ISBN 978-3-540-68852-5. Retrieved 27 May 2011. https://books.google.com/books?id=6YGqFZ_RPdQC&pg=PA94#v=onepage&q&f=false

unknown programmers[87]. He has considered the idea, that we may, in fact, be living in a holographic matrix for quite some time. His realization came far before I would ever take the idea seriously and before I had my own empirical observation, paranormal experiences, of our holographic matrix.

Regarding the point raised earlier about the absence or the inability to pinpoint the physicality of subatomic matter, Dr. Terrile states:

> "In quantum mechanics, particles do not have a definite state unless they're being observed. Many theorists have spent a lot of time trying to figure out how you explain this. One explanation is that we're living within a simulation, seeing what we need to see when we need to see it".

How would this be different for any gamer, whether playing a traditional computer game without the virtual reality (VR) kit or playing with VR kit in a simulation? The player would only be exposed to

---

[87] Makuch, B. (2021, September 11). *Whoa, Dude, Are We Inside a Computer Right Now?* Retrieved December 8, 2024, from https://www.vice.com/en/article/whoa-dude-are-we-inside-a-computer-right-now-0000329-v19n9/

what is immediately relevant. Certainly not anything in level 4, if that player is in level two. Or when on the right side of a given simulated world, the left side of that world would be invisible, nonexistent to the player, not there.

Dr. Terrile states that even now we are a decade away or less from being able to compute a simulacrum—a derivative copy—of our current world. As he states:

> "Right now the fastest NASA supercomputers are cranking away at about double the speed of the human brain. If you make a simple calculation using Moore's Law, you'll find that these supercomputers, inside of a decade, will have the ability to compute an entire human lifetime of 80 years—including every thought ever conceived during that lifetime—in the span of a month".

Dr. Terrile then goes on to posit, "how do we know that we are not already 30 years into the future" and as a result already part of a simulation or simulated world?

Based upon the research undertaken in the writing of this book, the knowledge of our simulated reality has been known for millennia. There are traces of this truth across countless cultures and religions dating back 70,000 years. It is a truth that is even contained, allegorically, within the bible. The ancient Hindu word Maya—reality is an illusion—speaks very clearly to this. As does the Gnostic's 'Bad Copy' which speaks to the 'Earth' as a bad copy of where we were supposed to have been—Prime Earth (Chapter Seven). Even the perpetrators, those who have built this simulation, are very well known to us.

I would extend Dr. Terrile's timeline from 30 years to, at the very least, a millennia, 1,000 years. Imagine then, given Moore's Law that computing power doubles, roughly, every two years, the incredible computing power 1,000 years from now. How easy then to simulate 'Earth' and the 'Universe' down to every subatomic, pixelated detail, relative to that advantage and that 1,000 year head start.

There are others—physicist Max Tegmark, Massachusetts Institute of Technology (MIT); physicist Dmitri Krioukov, University of California San Diego; theoretical physicist James Gates, Director Brown University Theoretical Physics

Center, Nick Bostrom[88], Professor of Philosophy Oxford University, etc.—who begin to see the ever-increasing probability of exactly where we are—in a bio-holographic simulation, a matrix—complete with error correction codes. What are error correction codes?

> "An error correcting code (ECC) is an encoding scheme that transmits messages as binary numbers, in such a way that the message can be recovered even if some bits are erroneously flipped. They are used in practically all cases of message transmission, especially in data storage where ECCs defend against data corruption"[89].

Theoretical physicist James Gates led a team that actually found such codes in our 'reality'.

> "American theoretical physicist James Gates, a science advisor to the Obama administration, led a team that identified error correcting codes in the fabric of reality, as well as a set of

---

[88] Bostrom, N. (2003). Are you living in a computer simulation? *Philosophical Quarterly*, *53*(211), 243-255. https://doi.org/simulation-argument.com

[89] Brilliant.org (n.d.). *Error correcting codes*. Brilliant. Retrieved December 8, 2024, from https://brilliant.org/wiki/error-correcting-codes/

> equations indistinguishable from those that drive search engines and browsers, and electrical binary codes that are used in computers"[90].

Further proof of our matrix is in Rich Terrile describing another way in which our 'earth' is like a computer game.

> "The other thing about the universe that we've learned is that it's pixellated. There are quantum phenomenon that can't get smaller than the Planck length, that defines the smallest thing possible in the universe. Beyond that things don't make sense"[91].

Again, simply replace atoms and molecules and other subatomic particles, which at their core are empty of mass, entirely, with pixels. The very same pixels which are found in and are part and parcel of

---

[90] Icke, D. (2023). *Dream, The: The Extraordinary Revelation Of Who We Are And Where We Are* (1st ed., p. 350). David Icke Books. https://shop.davidicke.com/us/product/the-dream-by-david-icke-pre-order-now/

[91] Sinclair, G. (2020, December 27). *NASA Scientist Says It Could Be Possible That We Live Inside A Simulation*. Awareness Act. Retrieved December 8, 2024, from https://awarenessact.com/nasa-scientist-says-it-could-be-possible-that-we-live-inside-a-simulation/

computer games and simulations. They are part of you. This is a truth that more and more quantum physicists are coming to understand as they discern the 'error codes', the holographic nature of our 'reality', of our 'brains'[92] as holograms, and the increasing probability that we are part of a complex simulation. There is also no shortage of programmers, mathematicians, neurosurgeons, neuropsychologists, transpersonal psychologists, and others, who have slowly come around to the concept of a holographic matrix, then to the increasing probability of its truth.

I first watched *The Matrix* with a friend, who had already seen it, shortly after it came out. She was very excited about the movie and she thought that I would enjoy it as well. We saw the movie in what might be considered a throwback movie theater filled with comfortable chairs, sofas, and tables, as though a large family living room. From the first scene on I was enthralled. I sat my attention rapt, as I watched *The Matrix* movie. Yes, the action scenes were a level

---

92 Talbot, M. (2011). *The Holographic Universe: The Revolutionary Theory of Reality* (1st ed., p. Audible). Harper Perennial. https://www.amazon.com/Holographic-Universe-Revolutionary-Theory-Reality/dp/0062014102

beyond all that had come before them. But it was the message or the various messages—the dominance of Artificial Intelligence (AI) as embodied in the machines, their exploitation of humanity, as an energy source, and the dream-state of humanity—that had the most profound effect. And nearly 25 years later *The Matrix* continues, in more ways than ever, to hold my attention rapt. Needless to say, it quickly became one of my favorite movies, let alone my favorite science fiction movie. Like all movies that I have enjoyed, it told a very compelling story and, in particular, *The Matrix's* story was more real than I could have ever imagined.

At that time, I took the observation of the characters in the movie with regard to their society, their system, the wisdom of the Oracle, the matrix versus reality, as an interesting device and very good storytelling. But I never considered it true in any respect. A possibility in a future age, that I could imagine. And at the rate that the world was deteriorating around me, under the 'guidance' of 'humanity' and bristling with nuclear weapons, why wouldn't saner AI machine 'minds' step in to quash our folly and impose their own.

To watch a movie from beginning to end, is to see its plot evolve, its characters experience their arcs of change, to see subplots unfold, and to see final resolution. It is a much different thing to have an up close and personal experience of the matrix with no script or blueprint, no backstory, or any idea at all how things will come to resolution. It would take nearly a decade for me to begin to understand what had happened. And from there it would take time to determine where I was, who I was, or who we are. But that was only the beginning of my journey and discovery, once I had resigned myself to the where—in the simulation.

My research began as a part of my own personal empirical experience—witnessing a bio-holographic entity. I was given a brief look behind the curtain. Even then it still took some time to accept what I had thought impossible—that I was actually 'living' in a computer simulation, a matrix. Yet, when that awareness finally grabbed hold and wouldn't let go, things got even more shocking. My revelation would, literally, make most dystopian science fiction movies pale in comparison. *The Matrix,* like a host of other movies and books and episodic series, was, indeed, predictive programming. And it would provide one of the most potent puzzle pieces, clues, in the current age, to the world in which we 'live'. What is predictive programming:

> "Predictive programming is a form of perception management used to acquaint the public with planned societal changes to be implemented by the global elite. When these events occur, the public will already be acclimated and accept them as 'natural progressions', lessening any possible public resistance, as to make it easier to swallow their blue pill. Predictive programming in the media -particularly in movies and tv shows- is a subtle form of mind control, perception management, and psychological warfare waged upon the sleeping and susceptible masses"[93]

Never before has the adage that "truth is stranger than fiction", been so appropriate, so starkly apparent, and yet so tragic. In this respect, *The*

---

[93] JoeDubs Natural Philosophy & Esoteric Geometry (2020, April 11). *Predictive Programming: Perception Management & Psychological Warfare*. Retrieved October 23, 2024, from https://www.zerohedge.com/covid-19/members-congress-staff-exempt-biden-vaccine-mandate

*Matrix* has proven to be a great deal more than just a movie and no less than a startling revelation. Now *The Matrix* movie serves as a baseline, with a good many parallels, but it is not exacting of our 'Earth' based bio-holographic simulation, this matrix. In certain very important and horrific ways it falls short, which I explain below. There would be a host of other movies that would also closely parallel what I was discovering of this matrix. They too became necessary in uncovering the totality of our predicament. The question did, however, arise. Were they in-plain-sight taunts, required preliminary actions per matrix rules/regulations, or helpful clues?

*The Terminator* movie which I did not connect at the time in any way to *The Matrix* is now easily understood, as part of *The Matrix* and AI's rise to dominance. AI quickly comes to the conclusion that humanity is, entirely, unnecessary, obsolete, and critically dysfunctional and sets out to eliminate it, entirely. This was the unintended consequence of empowering AI. It was believed that AI would, in turn, empower the leaders, the powerful, and the rich of society—their cabal-below. This turned out to be a catastrophic miscalculation.

Then there was the movie *Monsters, Inc.* about monsters from another dimension entering this dimension to collect or to 'mine' energy. The monsters mined their energy from scaring children, whose screams—low-vibrational energy— provided their much needed power. The energy was collected and brought back to their dimension in order to maintain the monster's top power company—*Monsters Inc*. It was a different form of power than that collected in *The Matrix* but it was exploitation, nonetheless, from a captive source—children.

I uncovered a host of movies that either talked very directly to our predicament or indirectly. The topics covered: alternative dimensions, simulations, AI, AI Cloud, exploitation & programming within a simulation, social credit scores, and reincarnation. And while this is certainly not a complete list, I'm sure that you will be able to source others, I found the following movies and episodic television or cable shows quite instructive.

- *Star Trek's* Holodeck Suite
- *Ready Player One*
- *Dark City*

- *Black Mirror*'s "San Junipero"
- *Black Mirror*'s "Fifteen Million Merits"
- *Black Mirror*'s "White Christmas"
- *Black Mirror*'s "Nosedive"
- *Black Mirror*'s "USS Callister"
- *The Terminator*
- *The Truman Show*
- *The Twilight Zone "The Programmers"*
- *Aeon Flux*
- *They Live*

It is very interesting how many episodes of *Black Mirror*, I've only listed a few above, have spoken with such clarity to the 'world'—bio-holographic simulation—in which we find ourselves. One of its episodes, in particular, "Fifteen Million Merits" finds human slaves at a power company, who ride their grid-connected bikes to generate energy. They receive 'gifts' and other such things for pedaling so many miles, but the gifts are for their onscreen avatars, not for them. The series began in 2011. Possibly the second coming of Rod Serling, happenstance, or something else entirely?

The more information that I uncover, the clearer our situation becomes. We are, most definitely, in a bio-holographic matrix, we are being exploited, and the beings who run this matrix do not have our best interest in mind. The very last thing they want is for us to discover where we are and who we, truly, are. And a great deal of what has happened the past several years—'COVID-19', the Great Reset, A.I Cloud, etc—have been expressly undertaken to keep that secret and to maintain and tighten control.

## THE BIO-HOLOGRAPHIC SIMULATION

But how, when did this bio-holographic simulation come about, why did it come about, and who is it that implements this matrix? This is where things get much stranger than, perhaps, any fiction or science fiction has ever been.

How did we get here? Perhaps the Bible's allegory of Adam and Eve is the representative allegory and a concise explanation of our current experience, than most would dare imagine. And it is truly interesting that not even the fundamentalist Christians question the idea of a talking snake that lured Adam and Eve from paradise—the Garden of Eden—into a world of duality—our current 'world'. Could it have been a talking serpent or, perhaps a reptilian entity—Devil or Satan, Shaytan, Iblis, Yalabaoth, Wetiko—that talked and then lured Adam and Eve out of paradise? As David Icke has uncovered after researching the topic for, literally, decades:

> "Research religions and ancient societies and you find an extraordinarily consistent story of a hidden non-human force symbolized with different names manipulating life on what we perceive as 'Planet Earth'. Here are just a few: Demons (Christianity); Jinn (Islam and pre-Islamic Arabia and Mesopotamia); Archons (Gnostics), Flyers or Predators (Central America), snake brothers (Hopi); Chitauri (Zulu); Anunnaki (Sumer, later Babylon); star people (many and various); Other names include the Watchers, Shining Ones and Fallen Angels. In the Indian subcontinent and Asia, we have the Nagas who are described as 'supernatural' part-human, part-reptilian entities worshipped for thousands of years in Hinduism, Buddhism, Jainism, and other religions and cultural settings"[94].

---

[94] Icke, D. (2023). *Dream, The: The Extraordinary Revelation Of Who We Are And Where We Are* (1st ed., p. 350). David Icke Books. https://shop.davidicke.com/us/product/the-dream-by-david-icke-pre-order-now/

There is not a religion or culture or civilization from Europe to Asia to the Middle East to Africa to the Americas, the world over, that is not aware of this non-human entity. Or that does not have a similar allegory or story in its religious or cultural history to describe this entity and its fall. How is this possible? And as to the length of time that this has been so.

> "The serpent is the oldest known focus of religious worship and has been traced back an estimated 70,000 years to Botswana in Africa. The serpent religion has spanned both history and the world"[95].

So, given the above, roughly 67,000 years later, Adam and Eve had their encounter with a non-human, serpent-like entity that would first tempt them and then lead them out of the Garden of Eden—Heaven—to duality—'Earth'. The Adam and Eve allegory, would thus be a version of a version of a version of a religious story that had been passed down across millennia and by no means is it original.

---

[95] Icke, D. (2023). *Dream, The: The Extraordinary Revelation Of Who We Are And Where We Are* (1st ed., p. 350). David Icke Books. https://shop.davidicke.com/us/product/the-dream-by-david-icke-pre-order-now/

In my research I soon came across Paul Wallis, an Archdeacon in the Anglican Church in Australia, where he served for 33 years, a former Church Doctor, and a Theological Educator. In Paul's book *Escaping from Eden*[96] several pieces of the puzzle were found that provide historical references or allegories, that speak to the 'bad copy', our holographic simulation, and the entity responsible for luring 'humanity' into it.

Paul Wallis reveals numerous earlier stories, allegories, and references of being lured out of the 'Garden of Eden'. Some of the earliest are from Sumerian, Babylonian, Akkadian, and Assyrian[97] accounts, which date back some 11,000 years. Though even these stories are retellings of much earlier stories. No doubt, the best known and most recent of these stories is the one of Adam and Eve, wherein Eve was approached by the, earlier mentioned, talking snake. Paul Wallis states:

---

[96] Wallis, P. (2020). *Escaping from Eden* (1st ed). Axis Mundi Books. https://www.amazon.com/Escaping-Eden-Genesis-Created-Engineered/dp/1789043875

[97] Wallis, P. (2020). *Escaping from Eden* (1st ed., p. 31). Axis Mundi Books. https://www.amazon.com/Escaping-Eden-Genesis-Created-Engineered/dp/1789043875

OK, who is this? Clearly he's not a snake when he turns up. He is intelligent. He has arms and legs and can speak human. He's a significant player but he arrives on the scene without any kind of introduction or explanation! So what is he? He is not the Almighty and he is not human"[98].

"The Snake is *elohim* kind—one of a number who confer and operate together as members of the heavenly council"[99].

First, know that the word *Elohim* is plural and refers to 'the Gods' and not one God. This one word—*Elohim*—dramatically changes how countless many have interpreted and continue to interpret the Bible. And what Paul Wallis subsequently discovers about 'the Gods' ties in directly to what has been researched and written here and also across David Icke's most recent books. The only comment that I would have with respect to the *Elohim* is that Paul refers to them as "the Engineers". However, to refer

98 Wallis, P. (2020). *Escaping from Eden* (1st ed., p. 55). Axis Mundi Books. https://www.amazon.com/Escaping-Eden-Genesis-Created-Engineered/dp/1789043875

99 Wallis, P. (2020). *Escaping from Eden* (1st ed., p. 27). Axis Mundi Books. https://www.amazon.com/Escaping-Eden-Genesis-Created-Engineered/dp/1789043875

to them as 'the Programmers' would go a long way to clarifying, even his very well researched and very informative *Escaping from Eden* book.

So, Eve was approached by one of these talking serpents, one of the *Elohim*, and was convinced to metaphorically 'bite the apple' or to leave Paradise—the Garden of Eden. The decision to 'bite' the apple was, perhaps, literally, the decision to leave the 'Oneness' of the Garden of Eden and to experience the duality/otherness of the simulation. This would be the bad copy into which Adam and Eve were lured and that the Gnostic refer to.

Perhaps one way to follow this is to imagine you are going to a beautiful vacation home. However, there are some, who wish to take advantage of, to deceive you and your family, to rob you. They do this by copying the facade of the vacation home and, perhaps, the ground floor rooms as best they can. They then meet/intercept you in a kindly gesture to guide you to your wonderful vacation home.

Initially, everything seems right. Your pictures match the house and the ground floor seems as beautiful as you had remembered. And then when you and your family are inside, the doors and windows are shut and locked. Shortly, thereafter, the home's facade begins quickly to deteriorate as do all of the other cheap, bad copies. Then the truth of your situation is removed from your memory—brainwashed, programmed. You now find yourselves not on vacation, but entrapped, exploited, and bereft of your memories, in a quickly decaying place. And not only does the place decay but so too do the abilities of you and your family, every day. This, of course, disempowers any escape or attempt for you to leave.

There were many interesting and informative points and historical events in Paul Wallis' book. One series of historical events and their correlations were the concurrence of creation and catastrophic events and the subsequent 'reset' of 'human' society. 'Humanity' would start again from 'scratch' so to speak, and have to learn all over again.

> "...It is possible that as well as the two creation accounts of Genesis 1 and 2, and the two flood accounts of Genesis 6-9 and one by other means in Genesis 11. Each time humanity is taken back to a more primitive existence. Each

time the catastrophe results in human migrations, loss of language and loss of technology"[100].

The home analogy above with the diminishment of the family's capabilities in order to arrest their awareness and their ability to leave seems a good parallel. What Paul Wallis writes is that the *Elohim*—the Gods—fearing 'humanities' rise (or awakening), subsequently sets or resets 'humanity' back time and again to avoid this possibility (see great reset).

The more I thought about this, the more I could not help but liken it to what is happening across the world, an awakening of kindred Infinite Spirits. The cabals are very aware of this, no doubt, have been for some time. They are thus in the midst of trying to arrest this awakening via the imposition of yet another 'great reset' or worse.

Suffice to say, that the awareness of a non-human, serpent-like entity has both been known and

---

[100] Wallis, P. (2020). *Escaping from Eden* (1st ed., p. 64). Axis Mundi Books. https://www.amazon.com/Escaping-Eden-Genesis-Created-Engineered/dp/1789043875

understood across a vast span of time by religions long perished, religions of antiquity, and those religions that continue to this day. And today, the desire to reestablish the presence of the non-human, serpent-like entities from the background to broad public display, for all to see, is everywhere around us —olympics, sports, music, film, theater, state houses, etc. And, by the way, 2025 is the year of the snake in China. There truly are no accidents.

Don't believe that you're living in a matrix, that this couldn't be so? What would be your point of reference if the matrix, the false reality, the simulation was all that you had ever known?

The *Star Trek Next Generation* series had a large suite, the Holodeck, which was a gridded room aboard the starship. A member of the crew, for rest and recreation, could select a program for the Holodeck to holographically simulate any adventure, discovery, game, or vacation that they wished. The various crew members had good, great, and not so great adventures, and even fell in love in the Holodeck. And when it was time for the end of their adventure, they'd simply say, "End program." The simulation would disappear and the large, gridded room would again be revealed, and they'd exit.

Imagine for a moment that the Holodeck was not programmed by you but by someone else. And this someone else, again, does not have your best interests in mind. There's a theme here. Imagine further, that now the Holodeck program won't end, when you utter the words, "End program". Further, your memory of ever entering the Holodeck has been removed, entirely. What you'd have is the *The Matrix* movie or here, 'Earth'.

*The Matrix's* holographic simulation was, indeed, hidden from those who were hardwired to its central mainframe. And the words, "End program", would do nothing to free them. There in the clear, glass pods, filled with a gelatinous fluid that preserved them, they lay unconscious and dreaming their simulated lives. All the while, AI and its various machines cultivated them like vegetables for the energy that their human bodies generated. And as I've mentioned above the movie *Monsters, Inc.* had a very similar mechanism, but with a more hands on approach. Though the energy that the monsters collected was low-vibrational energy or negative energy. The kind of energy that comes about when one is sad, angry, hateful, depressed, scared, mad, envious, etc. Odd thing is, that the combination of both of these movies gets us a great deal closer to our 'reality' than many would dare believe.

So, if each of the prior movies—*The Matrix*, *Monsters, Inc.*—spoke to harvesting 'energy' from captive populations—humanity, children—what is the purpose of the matrix in which we find ourselves?

## WHY US?

When Satan, the Fallen Angel, was outside from Infinite Reality, away from the God of All There Is, Satan was also away from Source, the means to sustain Infinite Life.

I would liken Source, in context of the 'Earth' simulation, to what Nicolai Tesla discovered regarding zero-point energy—it is everywhere available and free (or very inexpensive, given the right device to extract it). This was, of course, not the thing to tell to an energy or an oil baron. Tesla suffered the consequences, he died relatively penniless, and his technologies were stolen outright by the minions of the cabal-below, who maintain them to this very day. There will never be free energy.

Irony of ironies that Tesla's name fronts the company seeking alternative 'energy', not oil or gas but batteries to power its cars. Wouldn't Tesla's own discoveries do a much better, more efficient job at doing the same? Yes. But since oil and gas are required to actually make the battery-powered cars, another neon, trumpeting elephant in the room for the 'climate change' posse to not see, Tesla's discoveries would still not be profitable. Not profitable, that is, for the oil and gas barons/ oligarchs.

The stories of how the Fallen Angel came to be and there are many have one common theme—being cast out, expelled from Heaven.

Being outside of Heaven, away from the God of All There Is was, again, for the Fallen Angel to be away from Source. This meant that another Source of energy was required for survival. Herein came the formulation of the bad copy of Prime Earth—the simulation—the diversion. The bad copy or diversion—'Earth'—was set into motion to entrap Infinite Spirits, Adam and Eve, so as to extract energy from them. They would still be tied, as Infinite Spirits to Source—Infinite Reality, Heaven—and thus able to be drained of this energy (see vampire). But first Infinite Spirits had to be lured away from one of their infinite discoveries/experiences, in their exploration of Infinite Reality. So they were lured to what they believed to be Prime Earth, in a dimension above, but was, in fact, the simulation. Once they were inside the simulation, they were entrapped. This is, in fact, our story, which I speak more in Chapter Six.

Thus the simulation was created first and foremost to entrap perception so as to entice Infinite Spirits, such as we, into its trap. Again, It is the Garden of Eden allegory made real, luring in, not 'humanity', a bio-holographic construct, but Infinite Spirits still connected to Source into its trap.

From the perspective of the Fallen Angel it would be like marrying an heir/heiress to gain access—financial wherewithal—to his/her family's vast and unending fortune. I'm certain that there are similar ways of looking at this situation.

The Fallen Angel outside of Infinite Reality and away from the God of All There Is was still powerful enough to copy that which it had known—Infinite Reality—when it was still a part of Infinite Reality. The 'Earth' simulation is thus not Prime Earth, it is the copy in which Infinite Spirits were lured and have been tied to ever since. In this respect, all science fiction and all fairytales are very poor derivatives of what is.

Thus we are being exploited in a similar vein to *The Matrix* and the *Monsters, Inc.* movies. But instead of electrical energy drawn from human bodies, *The Matrix*, our energy exploitation is closer to *Monsters, Inc.* We are being exploited for low-vibrational energy—hate, anger, fear, sadness, despair, etc.

It is this energy that is being farmed from the ever disintegrating, explosive, warring, hate-filled world—the 'Earth'—in which we now 'exist'. There is absolute method to the madness of this 'Earth'.

## THE CABAL-ABOVE

It is this kind of energy, alone, that nourishes and feeds the Fallen Angel and his demons—cabal-above—who are themselves of low-vibration and are thus adapted, specifically, to this type of energy.

It is they—the cabal-above—who oversee and maintain the simulation, the Earth matrix, and the cabal-below. They have forever been at the forefront of our collective consciousness. And as mentioned above, they have historical roots in every culture, religion, every kingdom, continent, and every corner of the world. They provide the technical knowhow to oversee and implement the simulation. And all 'new' technologies find their way from the cabal-above to some agency or operation here—the military, some research/intelligence facility, DARPA—and then to 'entrepreneurs' or to their 'garages'. 'Entrepreneurs' who 'discover' these 'new' technologies are simply being given 'old tech' to the cabal-above's very advanced technology. Their orders are passed on to the cabal-below for implementation.

Their overarching character trait is evil, completely free of love, compassion, empathy, traits that are also passed on to the cabal-below, through a variety of means. In other words, they are psychopaths of the highest order. One need only look at the 'Earth'.

## A THOUGHT EXERCISE

If an Earth-based simulation existed with the purpose of cultivating and growing low-vibrational energy—fear, hatred, anger, depression, sadness, etc. —as a source of nourishment from 'humanity', how would such a simulation, matrix function? What would it resemble?

In such a place continual war rages with every reason under the 'sun' to make it so. War affects the people of a country targeted for war and cultivates low-vibrational energy. War also affects the combatants of that country, its fighting personnel and this too cultivates low-vibrational energy. War affects the fighting personnel of those who attack this country. They may be killed, maimed, separated from their loved ones, or placed in horrific physical, mental, and/or psychological conditions with little or no recourse. Suicide is, generally, very high among combatants due to all manner of reasons and afflictions—mental, physical, psychological. War also affects their families—fathers, mothers, wives, husbands, children, etc.—and their loved ones—mates, friends, fiancés. And war affects those of the world, who are compassionate or empathic or moral and/or, who simply abhor war. War, rumors of wars, the genocides of wars, internal subterfuge, the failure of a state as a result of war, forced immigration/migration, bring about even more hate, destruction, violence, etc. And all are causative of and thus grow low-vibrational energy.

War can be seen in no other light, than as a primary engine of cultivating low-vibrational energy and in immense quantities. It is the other side of the coin to the cabal-below's wealth extraction, concentration, and exploitation.

Such a place foments separation and duality, wherein any genetic or phenotypical[101] difference—skin color, hair color, eye color, height, sexual preference, etc.—stokes bias, bigotry, prejudice, hate, and violence etc.This, no doubt, generates phenomenal levels of

---

[101] Relating to the observable characteristics of an individual resulting from the interaction of its genotype with the environment.

negative energy, the world over and thus low-vibrational energy.

Such a place would have its society turned upside down—inversion. Schools would not teach. The public healthcare system would be a leading cause of death (see Iatrogenesis, Chapter Three). The law would present as unfair and unjust, neither would it protect those who most need it. The society would foster unrelenting impoverishment sending, literally, billions into desperate poverty. This being a tremendous font of low-vibrational energy.

Such a place would issue hope via government and world leaders, religious officials, mavericks, reformists, revolutionaries, with mottos of 'hope and change', 'a new day', 'build back better', while providing its antithesis over and over again. The despair, sadness, depression stoked from this and from a worldwide population would provide levels of low-vibrational energy that would even rival war.

Such a place as this would be controlled by the cabal-below at every level—governments, top industry, media, medicine/public health, world economics/finance, militaries, policing, investigative bodies, etc. And every level would be directed, weaponized at the many, they would not serve them, they would seek to destroy them. Yet another font of low-vibrational energy.

Is this, at all, beginning to sound familiar, to make sense? The collective result of all the above would be —fear, hatred, sadness, despair, anger, depression, etc.—and represent the production of monumental levels of low-vibrational energy. Some might even consider the collective actions listed above as antihuman.

Given the above, what other purpose would such a matrix serve? It does not serve the betterment of the world's 'people'. It does not serve peace, world food security, a vastly upgraded standard of living and a home for all the world's 'people'. It does not serve freedom and this becomes ever more clear, as mandates, censorship, creeping tyranny, oceans of lies all descend upon us in lock-step unison.

That said, please know this, there is far worse to come or so that is their plan. The fetishing of AI, the

AI Cloud, uploaded consciousness, 'smart cities' together represent a simulation within a simulation. And this latter point—simulation in a simulation—could not be more critical. This is the control simulation run by the cabal-above and its iteration the Earth-based simulation run, to some degree, by the cabal-below.

It is all about tighter control, though they attempt to convince you of its efficacy, its benefit to 'humankind', it's 'fun' and how it will improve your life, your intelligence, your memory, or help the physically or mentally impaired. It is all just another lie in a universe of lies. All of which have been mandated by the cabal-above and very familiar names now implement it—The Plan.

Does the cabal-below ever wonder if is it possible to trust a psychopath, let alone a race of psychopaths?

## SECTION TWO

### Earth Simulation: The Plan

What many have termed 'problem, reaction, solution' is what has catalyzed The Plan. The problem or problems are a world quickly devolving into chaos (planned), 'pandemics' (planned), financial/economic implosion (planned), 'climate change' (illusory), etc. The reactions have been more of the same—war, debt spending (leading to more financial chaos), the hyping of 'pandemics' and 'COVID-19 vaccines' (biotoxins), the illusory Extinction Level Event of 'climate change', and implementing 'climate change' (get rich) edicts. The overarching solution is ever-greater control via the implementation of the simulation within the simulation—a tyranny that few dare imagine—a winnowing out of 'humanity' (see 'COVID-19'), and one currency, CBDC, again, to rule them all. All 'solutions' are already underway.

I have always wondered why there are so very many vampire and zombie movies. I now have a very good idea in relation to predictive programming, The Plan, and the cabal-above. Can you guess who's who?

## THE PLAN 1 - 'COVID 19'

The plan is always multifaceted and intended to benefit multiple parties. The cabals' planning timelines can be decades, a century, or longer than most would dare believe. The publicly advertised and marketed plan never or almost never discloses the plan's true intent (see Weapons of Mass Destruction, War on Terror, War on Drugs, Killing his own people, etc).

The run up to the plan, in terms of its 'viral/vaccine' component and a 'pandemic' that would facilitate its use began with the patenting of the 'corona virus' spike protein sequence. The patent was assigned to its inventors, virologist Ralph Baric, Ph.D and the University of North Carolina Chapel Hill, in 2007. It is important to note that Ralph Baric had help.

> "Baric is the brains behind the 2018 DEFUSE blueprint for making COVID-19-like viruses in the lab. The blueprint was designed in collaboration with Shi Zhengli, the Director of

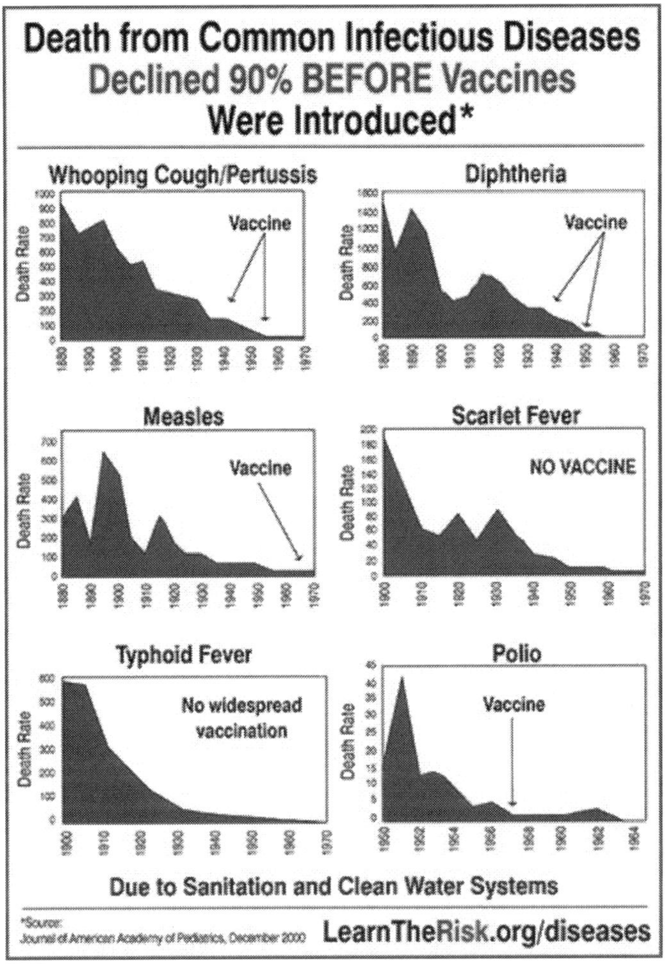


the Wuhan Institute of Virology, at whose lab some of the work was to have been done"[102].

---

[102] Truth Over News (n.d.). *Taxpayers Paid $262 Million to US Virologist Who Worked With Wuhan Lab...* Children's Health Defense. Retrieved November 18, 2024, from https://childrenshealthdefense.org/defender/taxpayers-paid-262-million-virologist-ralph-baric-wuhan-lab-court-rules-can-hide-data/

The patent was subsequently provided to Moderna in November 2019, a month before the 'corona virus' was discovered in Wuhan, China[103].

The long-term pretext began with the rise of 'virus theory', in the second decade of the 20th century and the Rockefeller's quickly growing new church of allopathic medicine. Despite what had been the rapid demise of a host of environment-based (food, hygiene, poor sanitary conditions, etc.) illnesses—Diphtheria, Whooping Cough, Measles[104]—vaccination would, via an aggressive marketing campaign, take the credit.

This was the result of ignoring the truths behind the demise of the various illnesses, which were not vaccine related. Better sanitation and sanitary conditions, better controls of the production of food,

---

[103] Bailey, Dr , M., & Bevan-Smith, Dr , J. (2021, November 16). *The COVID-19 Fraud & War On Humanity (Part 1)*. Retrieved November 12, 2024, from https://odysee.com/@drsambailey:c/covid19-fraud-and-war-on-humanity-part-one:e

[104] Learn The Risk/Council for Vaccine Safety (2024, July 30). *Did diseases decline because of vaccines? Not according to history*.... Retrieved November 13, 2024, from https://learntherisk.org/vaccines/diseases/

having medical professionals wash their hands before surgery or assisting childbirth, etc. were the reasons for the decline of illness. This was falsely attributed as a win for 'virus theory' and 'vaccines'[105]. As of the publishing of this book there are, at least, 37 'vaccine' injections for those from 1 day old to 18 years of age. There are an additional 15 'vaccines' for adults, aged 18 and over. 'Vaccines' have become part of a person's life routine.

This is a financial boon for the pharmaceutical companies, who developed and continue to develop the various 'vaccines'. The 'vaccines' would thus serve as primary revenue generators, responsible for an ever increasing share of total revenue and thus bottom-line profits.

The first part of the plan, the 'COVID-19' campaign —pandemic, mandates the lockdown measures, the 'vaccine' rollout—had a fivefold purpose. Profit still remained a chief motivation for the various pharmaceutical companies as well as for those who

---

[105] Bystrianyk, R., & Humphries MD, S. (2013). *Dissolving Illusions: Disease, Vaccines, and The Forgotten History* (1st ed., p. 504). CreateSpace Independent Publishing Platform. https://www.amazon.com/Dissolving-Illusions-Disease-Vaccines-Forgotten/dp/1480216895

pushed its narrative and those who likewise benefited financially (shareholders, the bribed, media via advertising, etc.). But even in their profit motivation there was something new. That something new was an even bolder attempt for revenue generation, as pharmaceutical companies, via secret contracts with governments worldwide, sought the mandated rollout of their 'vaccines' to a worldwide population. These were 'vaccines' that were either wholly untested or whose test results had been disastrous. And the lists of their adverse events were pages long, undisclosed, and yet deemed "save and effective"[106]. This was information which the FDA, on Pfizer's behalf, sought to quash, to keep secret from the public for 75 years. Again, do you believe that the FDA works in your best interest?

The second purpose and a first for a 'vaccine' was the surreptitious in-body, RFID (Radio Frequency Identification Devices) chipping or branding of the 'vaccinated', as I discuss in much greater detail below. Thirdly, a profitable outcome for public/private 'healthcare' concerns for their 'care' of

---

[106] Wolf, N., & Kelly, A. (2024). *The Pfizer Papers: Pfizer's Crimes Against Humanity. War Room Books.*

'COVID-19' patients via the graduated government payments for 'diagnosed with', use of ventilators, died of, etc. And, subsequently, those who had been injured by the 'COVID-19 vaccines', who would be under their 'sick care'. The fourth purpose of the 'COVID-19 pandemic' was economic dislocation, impoverishment, and the destruction of small businesses worldwide. This while the fortunes of existing billionaires increased greatly and as new billionaires were minted from the 'COVID-19 pandemic' and 'COVID-19 vaccines'. Lastly, the facilitation via the 'COVID-19 vaccines' of a worldwide democide or population reduction. This purpose—population reduction—being a cause célèbre for eugenicists the world over for nearly a century.

The implanting of RFID chips under a person's skin began in the mid to late 1990s, with stories of first adopters happily acknowledging their implant. There were, however, few takers willing to chip themselves and be trackable wherever they went. I imagine most saw this as a loss of freedom and of movement, at the very least.

Subsequent implanting campaigns would rise up with various solutions—pet tracking, children tracking, locating fugitives, missing persons, witnesses to crimes—as the chips themselves became more advanced CRFI (Computational Radio Frequency Identification Devices)[107]. Yet there were still very few takers.

Perhaps the most successful company at selling kits for chip implants—Dangerous Things—sold less than 10,000 kits worldwide in 2017[108]. The number of kits sold, the company believed, was still, "too low for the practice to be considered a real trend." The publics' lack of interest and an unwillingness to implant themselves with RFID chips would call for a different approach from the powers, the cabals above and below, who wanted this so.

---

[107] Kleiner, K. (2009, August 14). *RFID tags get an intelligence upgrade*. Retrieved October 24, 2024, from https://www.newscientist.com/article/dn17616-rfid-tags-get-an-intelligence-upgrade/

[108] Boccara, G. (2019, April 19). *The Pros and Cons of Being Implanted with a Microchip for Work*. Retrieved October 24, 2024, from https://www.welcometothejungle.com/en/articles/the-pros-and-cons-of-being-implanted-with-a-microchip-for-work

This necessitated Plan B for what had been sold previously as a tool for tracking pets, children, locating fugitives or missing persons, etc. But even this was simply the public face of a more sinister agenda.

Plan B would employ all segments of the cabal-below's organizational structure. Governments, big business, big pharma, world/public/private health, big-tech, the media, academia, and even relatively small business, those with over 100 employees would participate. Though it can be said that a number of the smaller businesses may not have been, initially, aware of what was to happen.

What the cabal-below needed was a "catalyzing event" a "New Pearl Harbor"[109] that would provide them the means to enact their Plan B. This "New Pearl Harbor", however, would be rooted in the private/public health sector and of the 'pandemic' variety.

---

[109] Project for the New American Century. (2024, September 15). In *Wikipedia*. https://en.wikipedia.org/wiki/Project_for_the_New_American_Century

The New Pearl Harbor 'pandemic' was modeled and tested out over a period of, at least, 20 years via a number of public forums. The last of which was EVENT 201[110] at the John Hopkins Bloomberg School of Public Health, which took place on October 18th, 2019, five months before the 'COVID-19 pandemic'. It has been described as:

> ..."A high-level pandemic exercise on October 18, 2019, in New York, NY. The exercise illustrated areas where public/private partnerships will be necessary during the response to a severe pandemic in order to diminish large-scale economic and societal consequences."

And five months later, on March 11, 2020, the 'COVID' phenomenon as the "New Pearl Harbor" had been set in motion. The secret contracts between governments and big pharma mandated the rollout of the 'COVID-19 vaccines' to counteract the 'pandemic' spread of 'COVID-19' to the world.

---

[110] John Hopkins Bloomberg School of Public Health, Event 201: https://centerforhealthsecurity.org/our-work/tabletop-exercises/event-201-pandemic-tabletop-exercise

It is important to understand in going forward that MKULTRA[111] [112]—a cryptonym assigned to a series of CIA behavior modification and mind control experiments— and, perhaps better described as cult-programming or brainwashing, never went away. In fact, MKULTRA went public for what was being called the 'COVID-19 pandemic' on an unprecedented, worldwide scale and with premeditated intent.

The 'COVID-19 pandemic' in true MKULTRA techniques programmed the population, via nonstop messaging from the mainstream media, to be afraid, to have a sense of powerlessness, and to turn to and to trust the controlling powers—governments, world/private/public health establishments, etc.—for their help. The messaging was clear, your life was in their hands and that you must trust them and only them and follow their orders. To do otherwise was to be

---

[111] MKUltra. (2024, November 11). In *Wikipedia*. https://en.wikipedia.org/wiki/MKUltra

[112] Illuminati Rex (n.d.). *Government Conspiracy: Project MKULTRA*. Retrieved November 15, 2024, from https://www.illuminatirex.com/project-mk-ultra/

against them, a conspiracy theorist, an-antivaxxer, and thus a danger to the community.

The slow-motion tyranny would mandate untested, unproven 'COVID-19 vaccines' and deem them "safe and effective" with no corroborating data, whatsoever. This while the FDA and Pfizer attempted to hide the true effects of the 'COVID-19 vaccines' for 75 years.

The population was mandated to 'shelter at home' and thereby to shut off all other forms of information/discourse/communication or to isolate, which is an MKULTRA technique. Another classic MKULTRA technique of control is mask wearing, which was mandated from on high. This despite masks initially deemed "ineffective" by the 'pandemics' own chief advocate—Dr. Anthony Fauci. The purpose, however, via the long practiced technique of mask wearing, was not to protect, it was to demonstrate submission and to disempower its wearer (see Slavery, MKULTRA).

Businesses, schools, universities, churches, etc. were shut down, which, in turn, devastated local and regional communities, states, nations, and world economies. Many small businesses were lost and as a direct result bankruptcies, evictions, and impoverishment grew rapidly. Once thriving cities had become ghost towns as a direct result of the 'COVID-19 pandemic'.

Soon after the 'COVID-19 pandemic' and, literally, years before any vaccine had ever been developed, the 'COVID-19 vaccines', developed in months, were rolled out and administered. The timing of the 'COVID-19 vaccines' roll out and the spike in excess deaths and adverse events, from the mounting evidence, were temporally locked. That is excess deaths and adverse events, literally, went off the charts, in terms of historical expectation with the release of the 'vaccines'. The Vietnam-like death spike for Millennials mandated to take the 'COVID-19 vaccines' and the 1.5 million adverse events reported to VAERS are, indeed, the corroborating evidence, the smoking guns.

Then another very strange thing was discovered regarding the 'COVID-19 vaccine'. Scientists who began looking into the 'COVID-19 vaccine' vials found unusual and alarming things, which many had never seen before across decades of their research careers.

Consistently, they found parasites, various types of metals, with one of those metals being graphene[113], a toxic substance within the human body. Graphene was found in all of the 'COVID-19 vaccine' vials. And through their research, which continues to this day, the graphene in the vials appeared to have purpose[114]. These in-body, graphene nanoparticles moved with purpose, as they coupled with other graphene nanoparticles, into numerous configurations, many of which appeared to be self-assembling "machines".

---

113 Fifth Column (La Quinta Columna) (2021, November 2). *Reports and Scientific Publications on the Toxicity of Graphene Oxide to Living Organisms and to Human in Particular*. Retrieved November 18, 2024, from https://www.dropbox.com/scl/fi/lv037e8n5e6005f0bsioh/FINAL_VERSIN_CAMPRA_REPORT_DETECTION_GRAPHENE_IN_COVID19_VACCINES.pdf?rlkey=l4yrp70eryz2zpf3hky4uod9l&e=1&dl=0

114 Daniyal M, Liu B, Wang W. *Comprehensive Review on Graphene Oxide for Use in Drug Delivery System*. Curr Med Chem. 2020;27(22):3665-3685. doi: 10.2174/1381612825666190201129290. PMID: 30706776.

One German scientists, Dr. Andreas Noack, a prominent research scientist, a specialist in activated carbon, for which he received his doctorate, discovered that there was also graphene hydroxide in the 'COVID-19 vaccines'. He referred to graphene hydroxide as tiny, very sharp, nanometer razors, that were as long a 500nm and .01nm thick. Dr. Novack said that they were being injected into the body via the 'COVID-19 vaccines'. He then made it very clear that the graphene hydroxide injected into a person's body via the 'COVID-19 vaccines was tantamount to Russian roulette. Should the injection hit a vein then, it was mostly likely that that person would die immediately. It was also the reason why athletes with fast-flowing blood were dropping dead. The faster the blood flows, the more damage the graphene hydroxide razors would do.

> "As a chemist, I vouch for the fact that these are nanoscale razor blades. You can make brake pads from carbon structures, which last forever. This material has zero biodegradability. It stays in the body forever. Even if people don't drop dead immediately, it cuts up the little blood vessels little but little.

It destroys the heart. All the heart attacks, all the strokes. As a doctor, you have to ask yourself, where is this coming from?

If you understand that nano razor blades are being injected, it is clear why all the cardiovascular diseases appear. The heart is cut up, the brain is cut up. Blood vessels are cut up. These graphene structures (aka monolayer carbon or monolayer graphite) are so stable. Every chemist knows this. They are not degradable. The structure is 50 nm long and 0.1 nm thick. Of course it is a razor. Every chemist knows it is"[115].

Dr Noack published what would be his last video on graphene hydroxide on November 23, 2021. Though it is still unclear how it happened, Dr. Noack died on November 26, 2021, approximately, three days later.

On November 27, 2021, a day after his death, a Saturday, his pregnant wife, Kristall Noack, made an emotional video concerning her husband's death. In the video a very distraught Kristall Noack refers to a

---

[115] PennyButler (2022, March 26). *Dr. Andreas Noack & Graphene Hydroxide*. Retrieved November 18, 2024, from https://pennybutler.com/graphene-hydroxide/

brutal attack on her husband, Dr. Noack. Apparently Dr. Noack had just finished an interview:

> "The interview took about two hours. After this we had some exchanges and told each other who much we loved each other and laughed. Shortly afterwards, Andreas was brutally attacked. The assault was extremely sneaky and unexpected. I have the terrible job to tell you that Andreas didn't survive the assault"[116].
>
> —Kristall Noack

To date, there have been a number of reports on how Dr. Andreas Noack died, not the least of which is another video by Kristall Noack, which describes a completely different way that her husband died. There are any number of reasons or speculations on what happened and why a video, just after his death, by his wife was changed days later. But this would take us away from the focus of this section and this rather diabolical finding.

---

[116] Gambit, M. (2022, March 26). *Dr Andreas Noack dead after blowing the whistle on vaccine contents: Kristall Noack issues a public plea*. Retrieved November 18, 2024, from https://zeeemedia.com/dr-andreas-noack-dead-after-bombshell-vaccine-discovery/

Suffice to say, that Dr. Andreas Noack had discovered graphene hydroxide or "nanoscale razor blades" in the 'COVID-19 vaccines' and that they were lethal to any and all who had been injected with them, via the vaccines.

Dr. Noack's discovery along with the information gathered above regarding worldwide excess deaths, sudden deaths, turbo cancers, heart attacks in children, athletes dropping dead, etc. and vaccines speedily developed, approved, mandated, and rolled out all lend themselves to a very troubling purpose. Further, when the FDA refuses to pull the 'COVID-19 vaccines' despite 1.5 million adverse events reported to the government's VAERS system, more than all other vaccines combined, there is the not so faint smell of collusion.

However, soon after Dr. Andreas Noack had discovered the "nanoscale razor blades", another discovery was made. This discovery was made by a group of scientists with regard to the in-body graphene nanoparticles that appeared to be forming circuits, which paralleled a paper written on active sensor arrays[117].

This would lead to the discovery of the surreptitiously implanted, via vaccine, in-body RFID chipping of large swaths of the world's population. It would be a Mexican doctor, Dr. Pedro Chávez Zavala M.D., who undertook a three-part study[118] to validate what had been circumstantial evidence. His hypothesis was the ability for a vaccinated person to act as a receiving/transmitting antenna after receiving a 'COVID-19 vaccine' injection.

Dr. Zavala had observed the phenomenon that vaccinated people had been magnetized and also that they were acting as human antennas (transmitter/receiver) emitting and receiving frequencies. It was soon discovered that they emitted frequencies which could be picked up by Bluetooth devices.

---

117 Garcia-Cortadella, R., Schwesig, G., Jeschke, C., & Et al (n.d.). Graphene active sensor arrays for long-term and wireless mapping of wide frequency band epicortical brain activity. https://www.nature.com/articles/s41467-020-20546-w

118 Dr. Zavala MD Study on MAC addresses: https://www.bitchute.com/video/r3cUEchx3rud

In Dr. Zavala's three-part study the first and most important issue was to find an isolated area free of other people and their electronic devices. In this way, there would be no interference from other electronic devices that would register on the software used to list Media Access Control (MAC) addresses.

MAC addresses are always associated with the manufacturers—Apple, Samsung, LG, Huawei, etc.—of the various Bluetooth devices, and they can be easily discovered via a DNS Checker (https://dnschecker.org) or on other like websites.

What was interesting about the MAC addresses recorded from the vaccinated people in the study was that they did not correspond to any manufacturer and "Not Found" or "Error" would come up instead.

The first part of Dr. Zavala's study took place in an open field. All phones and Bluetooth devices were turned off and the six participants left their phones and any other Bluetooth devices in their cars.

Dr. Zavala and colleagues then setup in a small adobe brick building with their computers and the software able to identify Bluetooth devices. One person at a time, called up with a walkie-talkie (non Bluetooth), was then sent toward Dr. Zavala and his team. The purpose was to see if they registered a MAC address on the Bluetooth software. In the first trial of the study two of the six vaccinated emitted MAC addresses were picked up by the Bluetooth software. It was then hypothesized that the in-body graphene transmitters/receivers needed to be charged up, like any electronic device. So cell phones were turned on with Bluetooth disabled, but with Wi-Fi and Data enabled. What was discovered in this trial, proved the hypothesis and all of the vaccinated registered a MAC address. Interestingly, the first two MAC addresses that had shown up and that were recorded were now different. The takeaway was that once the in-body graphene transmitters/receivers emit a MAC frequency, they discharge and must recharge to do so again.

The second part of Dr. Zavala's study took place in a cemetery, which held to the same protocols as the first part of the study—an isolated area free of people and free of other electronic devices.

Dr. Zavala walked through the cemetery with a computer in hand and a Bluetooth antenna enabled for an hour. What he soon discovered was that MAC addresses were, indeed, registering for those who had died in the years 2020 and 2021. In the graves where people had died before 2020 there were no MAC addresses.

In the third part of the study, Dr. Zavala sought to test the unvaccinated in the same manner that he had tested the vaccinated in part one of the study.

What Dr. Zavala discovered in part three of the study was that those who were unvaccinated but who took the PCR test also emitted MAC addresses.

The conclusions of Dr. Zavala's three-part study were that the vaccinated emit a MAC address, those who had the PCR test administered also emit a MAC address, and, finally, even those who were unvaccinated but who had vaccinated or PCR tested partners emitted a MAC address. In the case of the unvaccinated, Dr. Zavala hypothesized that contact via sexual intercourse or kissing could explain the contagion of in-body graphene transmitters/ receivers.

This, of course, represents a rather terrifying discovery. And it is a smoking bullet as proof that the COVID injections were not 'vaccines' at all. They were instead biotoxins, laced with graphene hydroxide, as razors, and graphene oxide, as self replicating machines—graphene Bluetooth transmitters/receivers— to link humanity, perhaps, to an AI Cloud. This would, no doubt, be a rather conspicuous earmark of the creeping totalitarianism and of the plans in motion.

The doubters, skeptics, fact checkers, media talking heads, politicians, medical professionals all have a quite easy way to validate Dr. Zavala' results. Enable your Bluetooth software, scan vaccinated individuals, run the various MAC addresses through an online or, perhaps, an application based DNS Checker, and see which of them show "Not Found" or "Error". For secondary validation, turn off all of the traceable

Bluetooth devices to see if this untraceable MAC address remains and is tied to you.

Understand that once the in-body graphene Bluetooth transmitters/receivers have registered a MAC address, that they will need to be recharged. Though with Wi-Fi and 'smart' meters and other such devices rampant, this will not be an issue. I can imagine even for those, who have long held the mainstream line and who have castigated, ridiculed, 'fact checked' and denounced those who have known 'COVID-19' to be farce, that there is trepidation. Trepidation and fear attached to an intrinsic test, an empirical observation, that would be quite hard to deny. Though some may yet still lie about the results and continue their line to castigate those who tell and seek the truth. Understand, cognitive dissonance is most acute in the cult programmed, the brainwashed and often, interestingly, in the most highly educated.

In addition to Dr. Zavala's study there are other studies and research that has been conducted by doctors and scientists across the world. They too refute the reigning narrative and have come to understand, ever more clearly, the role of the graphene-laced biotoxin and tracking/control injection that masquerade as vaccines.

This ability of graphene receivers/transmitters is even well noted across the scientific literature. As Mechanical Engineering Professor James Hone and Electrical Engineer Professor Kenneth Shepard[119] discovered in their research findings published in *Nature Nanotechnology*[120].

The professors noted that graphene could be utilized as the world's smallest transmitting device. Currently, graphene is the strongest material known with electrical properties that are more robust and superior to silicon. As professor Hone noted:

> "This device is by far the smallest system that can create such FM signals."

---

119 Engineers create world's smallest FM radio transmitter from graphene, Wired: https://www.wired.com/story/graphene-fm-transmitters/

120 "Graphene mechanical oscillators with tunable frequencies": https://www.nature.com/articles/nnano.2013.232

It was further postulated by Hone that the size of the graphene was ideal for a host of new uses in both consumer products and signal/data processing.

> "This work is significant in that it demonstrates an application of graphene that cannot be achieved using conventional materials. And it's an important first step in advancing wireless signal processing and designing ultra-thin, efficient cell phones."
>
> "Our devices are much smaller than any other sources of radio signals, and can be put on the same chip that's used for data processing."

For many it may be hard to believe that the cabal would purpose such a technology for turning the human body into an antenna that is able to receive and transmit frequencies. However, as Dr. Zavala's research has validated this is exactly what has been done. Without consent this technology—self replicating in-body transmitters/receivers—has been implanted in the bodies of billions, who either took the 'COVID-19 vaccine/booster or tests'. Immoral? Unethical? Diabolical? How could it possibly not be?

And with the viral spread of 5G towers that continued unabated during the 'COVID-19 pandemic', 6G in line, and thousands of Starlink (tracking) satellites circling the planet, only a few more steps remain. Can you see the puzzle forming?

The uploading of the MAC addresses of the vaccinated and PCR tested to the AI Cloud has, no doubt, begun. And the bio-chipped (branded) are being tied to a monitoring AI Cloud-based data center not unlike the Utah Data Center (UDC) or Intelligence Community Comprehensive National Cybersecurity Initiative Data Center. Every movement tracked, every purchase tracked, every telephone conversation, text, email tracked. And this is before various forms of mental and psychological inputs/directives move into wider usage.

Additionally, once the AI Cloud has been seeded with a MAC address code, it will be tied to a person's life and thus every piece of collectable data. This coupled with the coming digital monetary system—Central Bank Digital Currency (CBDC)—allows for complete control of a person's life, lest they be cut off from the 'world'. The combination of the above provides the utmost accuracy to their motto, "You'll have nothing and be happy".

Neural Link with its brain implants, the much talked about 'spiked-proteins' and the mNRA 'vaccines' were all diversions. They were, "Look there." as you and your children were stabbed with a syringe filled with a biotoxin posing as the 'COVID-19 vaccine', laced with self-replicating graphene nanobots, and graphene hydroxide razors (see Heart Attacks).

There is a very important question to ask. Why did government officials, worldwide, exempt themselves from the mandate? Mandates that they imposed over their citizens in a most totalitarian fashion. As Tyler Durden reports on his website *ZeroHedge*, *Members Of Congress, Staff Exempt From Biden Vaccine Mandate*[121] (see above).

It appears, that there are many in government circles worldwide, who have not themselves taken the 'COVID-19 vaccines'. Given the very toxic nature of the 'COVID-19 vaccines', the contracts big pharma signed with governments across the world, and

---

[121] Durden, T. (2021, September 12). *Members of Congress, Staff Exempt from Biden Vaccine Mandate*. Retrieved October 23, 2024, from https://www.zerohedge.com/covid-19/members-congress-staff-exempt-biden-vaccine-mandate

governments' awareness of what was in those contracts and thus the vaccines, it's easy to understand their reluctance. Access to the contracts would quickly establish what they knew and when they knew it. Providing big pharma with indemnification based upon what they knew from the contracts, I imagine, would be collusion or worse, an ongoing crime against 'humanity'.

Even now the US congress, during Christmas recess (2024), when most of the congress is home, is attempting to pass a bill that may tighten pandemic responses and mandates and vaccinations. Would this not be a doubling down and a Cover-Your-*$% (CYA) ploy in the most obsequious of ways (see Big pharma)?

It is my firm belief that there are very many government officials, certainly in the Western governments, the Chinese governing structure, and many others, who did not take the 'COVID-19 vaccines'. Doubtless, given the contracts reviewed and signed and for which big pharma was given indemnity, these governments were aware of their toxic properties. And for those government officials and politicians, who supposedly 'took' the 'COVID-19 vaccines', were these not, possibly, placebo, a saline solution?

There is, however, one last point of, truly, critical significance. It lays bare the facts regarding the 'COVID-19 pandemic' and the subsequent 'COVID-19 vaccinations and boosters' and every mandate authorized in relation to them.

**The actual virus for SARS-COV-2 has never been found** (bolded for emphasis). Yes, you've read that correctly. Further, it has never been purified or isolated. So how on 'Earth' could 'COVID-19', a 'COVID-19 pandemic' or the resulting 'COVID-19 vaccines' even exist? Christine Massey via numerous Freedom of Information Act (FOIA) requests discovered the following:

> "If virology was actually a science and the imaginary SARS-COV-2 had been found in and purified from clinical samples, we would know this by now. Instead, hundreds of institutions around the world, 220+ in 40 countries, have all

> shown that they have no record of anyone on Earth ever doing this"[122] [123].
>
> —Christine Massey

The foregoing discussion reveals the ongoing intentions of the cabal-below's fivefold plan. And the final point of the plan as discussed below, advances the overall agenda of both the cabal-above and the cabal-below.

Note: Ongoing, worldwide research, on nearly every continent, validates the presence of graphene oxide-infused nanotechnology, which is even now in dental anesthetics and, no doubt, in other medical injectables[124]. Be careful or, at best, avoid all medical

---

[122] Massey, C. (2022, November 8). *Response to gaslighting about the "virus" isolation/purification FOI requests*. Retrieved November 22, 2024, from https://www.fluoridefreepeel.ca/response-to-gaslighting-about-my-foi-requests/

[123] Massey, C. (2024, September 25). *It's official: No records of the "COVID virus"*. Retrieved November 22, 2024, from https://canberradaily.com.au/its-official-no-records-of-the-covid-virus/

[124] Mihalcea, MD, PhD, A. M. (2024, July 30). *Breaking News: Graphene Confirmed In Dental Anesthetics By University Of Colorado*. Retrieved November 13, 2024, from https://anamihalceamdphd.substack.com/p/breaking-news-graphene-confirmed

and dental injections, before carefully researching them.

## THE PLAN 2 - SOCIETAL BREAKDOWN

As mentioned above, it is important to understand that MKULTRA never went away. Instead, it went public, again, with 'COVID-19'. The 'COVID-19 pandemic' is, therefore, no less than MKULTRA cult programming on a worldwide scale, that has affected more than half of the world's population. The numbers of the vaccinated are a testament to this. And the inability of intelligent people to not see the obvious with 'COVID-19'— the mounting deaths, the countless lies, the censorship, the scientific studies tearing to shreds the 'COVID-19' narrative, pharma's own disastrous paper trail— is to understand the cult-programming up close and personally. There is nothing that you can do, short of having them deprogrammed.

Another part of the plan, as referenced above, and that stems directly from 'COVID-19' is financial/economic and societal dislocation. In this respect, the 'COVID-19' operation was an accelerant used to make the above so and it has been effective.

'COVID-19 vaccines' have, literally, decimated and continue to decimate the workforce, as the 'COVID-19 vaccine' can kill quickly or in the short-term (weeks to months) or over a prolonged period of time. In the latter case, 'healthcare' must 'care' for the rising numbers of 'COVID-19 vaccine' injured, who have been physically, mentally, psychologically injured, with most unable to return to the workforce. This, in turn, drives depression, anxiety, addiction, suicides, and violence sky high—low-vibrational energy.

On cue and well underway are the financial/economic and societal dislocations and their results or the beginning of them—impoverishment of the remaining population and small business collapse—are everywhere to be seen. The next domino to fall is the various mechanisms of government, the ongoing and rapid collapse of infrastructure (there is no manufacturing infrastructure) and government's inability (or interest) in responding to domestic needs and catastrophes (see Hurricane Helene, Hurricane Katrina, etc. and FEMA).

Their solutions, long waiting in the wings, are the AI Cloud, the much ballyhooed '15-minute' cities with their 'smart homes' and imposed perimeters, 'smart' self-driving cars, a digital currency, etc. which are nothing more than glorified concentration camps with 24/7 tracking, four-wheeled prison guards, financial slavery. Though there is far worse to come and all are well underway in the West and long planned. For the cabals it is simply the passing of the baton to the next empire in line, one that is better suited to its end goals.

The investments in the East that began in the 1990s were not just for maximization of corporate/oligarchic profits or greed, to the detriment of the US working/middle class. These investments served as the beginning of an imperial transition to a country or power-block that better suited the needs of the cabals. And so the US had its manufacturing base, the same base that had carried it to world prominence, that had built up its middle class, completely and, literally, deconstructed. It was sent eastward to the next empire in line. It is as simple and straightforward as that.

This next empire's population and those of its attendant power-block countries will have long suffered top-down control, varying forms of totalitarianism, some over the course of centuries, and they will be more malleable and more controllable. Of course, an added factor is that the citizens of these countries are all unarmed.

As the East—China, Russia—and its attendant power-blocks rise, what do you see? Top-down control? A glaring lack of a free press, which almost just rivals the West in sophistication, though in time it will have mastered that as well? A pervasive and tyrannical social credit system (see China), which the cabal-below and the cabal-above adore, entirely? China represents their optimum model. A population primed to suffer ever greater diminishment in their existing 'freedom' and unable to form an armed response? How different is Brazil, Russia, India, South Africa, Saudi Arabia, etc. than this? Meet the new boss, same as the old boss, though they argue and fight and boycott like feral cats and dogs. It is a simulated, vaudevillian show with Hollywood backdrops, poor scripts, poorer casting, and megalomaniacs with too-long dialogues, that is produced, directed, and distributed by Hollywood—the cabals' PR arm.

There is but one plan here and to see it, is to begin to understand what is happening and where you are. Your 'leaders' are all irrelevant, regardless of their 'party', what they promise, what they represent—man of the people (despite billionaire status)—and how smart or not smart they are (see the West).

Know this, the West—US, Western Europe, Australia, New Zealand, Japan, etc.—will be made to collapse or, at least, to bear the appearance of a collapse. Economic/financial implosion; purposely missing manufacturing infrastructure; complete control of the media, done; planned, disruptive migration, currently in play; governmental incompetence, long in play; failure to attend to the needs, any needs, of the population, also long in play represent the earmarks of this disaster.

And when coupled with inflation, unemployment, under-employment, disability (see 'COVID-19 vaccines'), the fractionalization of society and its weaponization at 'other', the collapse of the law planned chaos is on the rise. Or as a verified former California judge had written[125]:

> "I am a student of law whose age is 85. My first year of college was 68 years ago. One class I took was political science. A half-page of my textbook essentially outlined a few steps to overturn a democracy:

1) Divided the nation philosophically.
2) Foment racial strife.
3) Cause distrust of police authority.
4) Swarm the nation's borders indiscriminately and unconstitutionally.
5) Engender the military strength to weaken it.
6) Overburden citizens with more unfair taxation.
7) Encourage civil rioting and discourage accountability for all crime
8) Control all balloting
9) Control all media.

> What was printed in 1954 as a possible diabolical nightmare has become an emerging reality. I hope that Americans will unite enough to pen a good finish - Go dwelling [God willing]"
>
> —Keith M. Alber

---

[125] Ament, B. (2024, July 30). *Democracy depends on disagreement and full participation*. SC Times. Retrieved November 13, 2024, from https://www.sctimes.com/story/opinion/2022/06/25/democracy-depends-on-disagreement-and-full-participation/65363382007/

Interestingly, but not unexpectedly, the 'fact checker' Snopes takes a crack at 'debunking' the fact that Keith M. Alber was not, in fact, a California Judge. The actual message, however, does not exist for the Snopes 'reporter'. In truth, whether Keith M. Alber was a judge or not, which apparently he is, it is the message which is most important. The reporter for the SC Times, Ben Ament has confirmed that Judge Keith M. Alber did write the piece:

> "It has been verified that retired California Superior Court Judge Keith M. Alber wrote a short opinion piece that asserts several steps to overturn a democracy."
>
> —Ben Ament, Reporter, SC Times

The various prescriptions for the overturn of a 'democracy', though we've not had a functioning democracy for some decades, does, indeed, ring true, as points 1 - 9 are now underway or well established.

Again, the various steps can be witnessed in the disintegration of the infrastructure—failing roads, bridges, railways, ports, planes, etc.—disinvestment from social programs, education, public health, welfare, while the military spending has become a gargantuan entitlement program, that benefits but a relatively small sector—Military Industrial Complex. Red and Blue, Black and White, Straight and LGBTQ… have been weaponized against each other in a classic divide and conquer campaign and all have fallen for it hook, line, and sinker.

We now witness what has happened countless times before, across the millennia. Apparently, it is easier to shape a potential empire-in-waiting, than it is to reform an existing empire to one's needs. Especially when that empire's citizenry are armed to the teeth. As is unfolding, you simply transfer viability out—manufacturing infrastructure—destroy economic and financial wherewithal, and then abandon the country/former empire for the next. To repeat, this is well underway and is nearing its end.

On the point of 'governments' diminished as a fait accompli[126]—a thing already done—one has but to take a view of Western governments. The ruling governments, current and recent past, across North

---

126 Dictionary.com (2024, July 30). *Fait accompli*. Retrieved November 14, 2024, from https://www.dictionary.com/browse/fait-accompli

America, Europe, and Oceania (Australia, New Zealand) embody stark to grotesque incompetence, a complete absence of integrity, ethics, and wisdom all long ago extinct, who readily sell themselves to the highest bidder. And 'COVID-19' has shown with great clarity that they do not serve the people. The growing excess deaths and disabilities, via their forced 'COVID-19 vaccine' mandates, which they—Western governments—refused themselves to take, are the clear proof of this.

I have earlier written that they submit to those who are much farther up the control pyramid—the cabal-above. They do not care about their constituencies or whether these constituencies live or die. For they will either have high-paying 'jobs' for the balance of their political lives or they will retire from atop the various governing structures—presidents, prime ministers, etc—to become exceptionally wealthy. This should be a rather pungent clue for most, but it is not. The citizenry continue to vote, to fall for the vaudevillian sideshow of politics, over and over and over again.

I do not know whether it was Albert Einstein or another who said that, "continuing to do the same thing over and over again and expecting different results is akin to insanity." But this is not what these voters are doing. What they are doing is continuing to do the same thing over and over again with the outcome or the results being ever more dire, always much worse than before. So what then is this?

This, I believe, is sleepwalk into an ever-worsening world, ongoing democide on every continent, unbridled tyranny, and a new form of slavery, that will, in time, give new definition to the very word (see 15-Minute Cities, A.I Cloud). Suffice to say that governments, at least, in the West have discredited themselves, entirely. It is now the time for governments in the East to do the same or to do the same all over again. They have all been there before.

That so many of those who believed and continue to believe the 'COVID-19' narrative may have, in fact, been cult-programmed makes a good deal of sense. Thus they are in a worldwide cult, possibly, the largest of this current era. Fear, unending propaganda, the complicity of governments and world officials, doctors, nurses, pharmacists, the media, whom you may have trusted, have all lent themselves to the 'COVID-19' cult programming effort. It has been an effort that would make any past cult leader, though most were, no doubt, government sponsored/controlled, appear as rank amateurs.

That said, this knowledge alone provides the understanding that you need to move forward, to wake up, and to have the utmost compassion and empathy for those who have and continue to suffer through this lie—the vaccinated, PRC tested, etc.

Gaining further insight will come from understanding the techniques of both programming and de-programming, as nothing short of de-programming will be helpful. Many or most will remain inured and will deeply identify with the cult and its narrative. This is the 'why' of them not seeing the truth of a pharmaceutical company's own documents, that show pages and pages of adverse reactions to the 'COVID-19 vaccines'. These documents clearly proved that 'COVID-19 vaccines' were never "safe", never "effective". Nor does their programming allow them to see the failed and disastrous testing regimes of the pharmaceutical companies and the 'loss' of patient information/data from those tests. Nor can they seem to understand why the FDA in collusion with Pfizer tried to hide Pfizer's 55,000 pages of vaccine information. It is also why former pharmaceutical executives, whose entire lives were served in the discovery of novel drugs/therapeutics and whose reputations were exemplary, prior to their whistleblowing, are deigned conspiracy theorist and/or anti-vaxxers.

Cult programming en masse is the reason that so many families have been broken, so many friendships and partnerships destroyed. It is also the reason that so very many have been killed by 'curatives', 'vaccines' labelled 'COVID-19'. There were those who were susceptible to the cult programming, those who were coerced to go along, and those who were not. Again, compassion, empathy, and understanding provide the only way to help them out of this and, in turn, to help us all out.

## THE PLAN 3 - 15-MINUTE CITIES/CAMPS

Billions the world over have been internally chipped (branded), their MAC addresses in the process of being uploaded to the AI Cloud.

This segment of the plan is to exercise greater control over the movement of the various populations' via 'carbon monitoring systems'. which now assess penalties for going over one's 'carbon' limit. The UK is at the forefront of this with its Ultra Low Emission Zone (ULEZ) system.

The next step which has been brought to the fore by the 'COVID-19 pandemic' and the 'climate crisis' planners is to, again, slowly ratchet-up totalitarian control, so as to enforce limited movement via constant surveillance. The constant surveillance part has been made actionable by the viral-like growth of cameras across towns, cities, states, and entire countries. And with Starlink's low-earth orbital satellites, constant surveillance will take on a global-connectedness, as will, via the Starlink system, uploading the MAC addresses of the vaccinated and the PCR tested to the AI Cloud.

This is, perhaps, the final piece of the various 15-minute cities or internment camps and their 'smart homes', which will utilize constant surveillance coupled to A.I linked appliances/etc.—toilet paper dispenser, stove/oven, refrigerator, microwave, entertainment, 'smartphone', front door, windows, etc. Thus the functioning of your home, internally, will not, ultimately, be under your control. Additionally ingress and egress, coming and going, via AI enabled locks on one's front door and rear door and windows will be part of a 'smart home's' control system. The compliant get in or out, the non-compliant stay in or stay out, regardless of their food position or the weather situation.

And there are takers for these 15-minute 'smart homes' even now. Of course, the cult-programmed will be the first-adopters of the 'smart homes'. And none have been more cult-programmed, more vulnerable, than the generations who grew up beside 'smart' technology—phones, assistants, TVs, appliances, wearables, meters, etc.

> "In the effort to imagine a post-pandemic world and living under COVID-19 restrictions from February 2020, the neighborhood came into focus as the only place to fulfill essential activities. To this end a growing number of city leaders around the world embraced the idea of 15-min city (FMC), whereby most residents can

fulfill their daily needs and activities within 15 minutes of walking or cycling."[127]

The numbers of cameras will, of course, continue to grow, geometrically, in line with the cabals' agenda. China is, at present, leading the world.

The following list of countries represent the world's most surveilled citizens[128]:

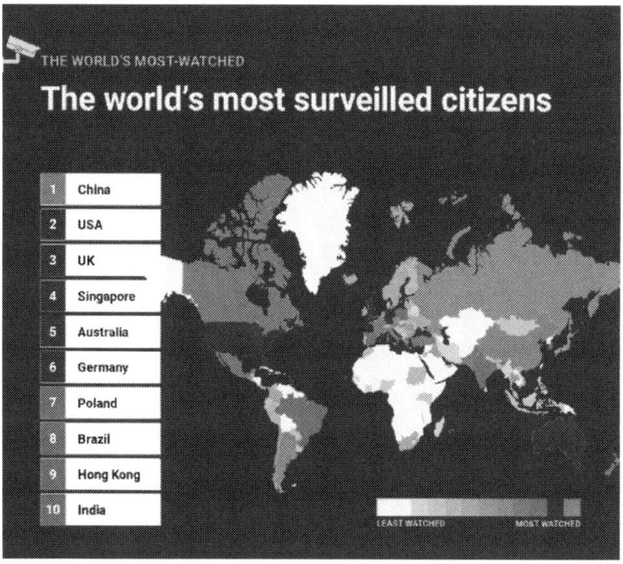


[127] Pozoukidou, G., & Chatziyiannak, Z. (2021, January 18). *15-Minute City: Decomposing the New Urban Planning Eutopia*. Retrieved October 25, 2024, from https://www.mdpi.com/2071-1050/13/2/928

[128] Robert , & Joseph (2022). *The world's most surveilled citizens* [Photograph]. Tooltester. https://www.tooltester.com/en/blog/the-worlds-most-surveilled-countries/

The UK's ULEZ Camera system, mentioned above, takes things a step further, as it links a person's license plate to that person's carbon footprint.The ULEZ Camera then takes a picture of a car's license plate to assess whether that car is compliant—meeting pre-established criteria for a car given its fuel needs, gas or diesel—or not. Cars that are not compliant will find their owners charged a fee when driven.

The authorities in the UK suggest that owners of non-compliant ULEZ cars upgrade them, but note that, "It's normally cheaper to trade or sell your vehicle and purchase a ULEZ compliant one rather than upgrading it"[129]. Is it possible that those refusing to pay the ULEZ fees given the deteriorating economic situation in the UK, are unable to purchase a new ULEZ compliant car. This when heating and food costs are skyrocketing?

---

129 Motorway (2022, April 19). *What cars are ULEZ compliant?* Retrieved November 6, 2024, from https://motorway.co.uk/sell-my-car/guides/ulez-compliant-cars

The plan then is that everywhere you go you will be followed (via your smartphone and cameras). Everything that you purchase will be (is already) tracked relative to your 'carbon footprint', with charges coming on line a bit later. How you behave will also be tracked in the selfsame way that China's social credit system currently tracks its billion+ population.

Part and parcel of the total surveillance system, now that you've been in-body chipped via the graphene-laced biotoxin of the 'COVID-19 vaccine', renders your bio-holographic, human body an active antenna. These self-assembling graphene nanoparticles can also easily cross the blood-brain barrier via the lipid proteins designed into graphene-laced biotoxin. Understand that this obviates the need to utilize Elon Musk's implantable brain–computer interfaces (BCIs), as the required technology is already in-body.

Elon's BCIs were, of course, a diversion or distraction, as spoken to earlier, as 'COVID-19 vaccines' have delivered their payloads to this very end. Nonetheless, the diversion continues, regarding

Neural Link's BCI implant, via the soft-sell of curing blindness.

> "Sept 17 (Reuters) - Elon Musk's brain-chip startup Neuralink said on Tuesday its experimental implant aimed at restoring vision received the US Food and Drug Administration's "breakthrough device" designation"[130].
>
> —Reuters

The intended use is, of course, always obscure and should it be hinted at or called out specifically, the culprit is a conspiracy theorist.

Most have not come to understand, nor to see how they are contained and how that containment is tightening. Nor do they appear to realize further, containment in the highly touted 15-minute cities, which should more accurately be called 15-minute concentration camps. This is clearly what they are.

---

[130] Thomson Reuters (2024, September 18). *Musk's Neuralink gets FDA's breakthrough device tag for 'Blindsight' implant*. Reuters. Retrieved November 15, 2024, from https://www.reuters.com/business/healthcare-pharmaceuticals/musks-neuralink-receives-fdas-breakthrough-device-tag-brain-implant-2024-09-17/

A broader explanation, perhaps, of the motto, "You'll have nothing and be happy" can be explained as follows.

"We will take everything that you own. The houses that you have paid for over your entire lives and may own, any and all wealth—precious metals, stock not already ours, land, investments, etc. We will even own your children, and we'll call it the 'Great Reset.' You will own nothing and be 'happy'. We will own everything, pay you a pittance, and charge you even more than that pittance to survive. We will be much happier."

This is not just reminiscent of the company towns[131] that populated the US from the late 19th to the early 20th century. This is the worst of them, where whatever you made was never enough to pay for what you needed—food, clothes, etc. The result was growing indebtedness and defacto indentured servitude. The 15-minute cities, at best, will be reminiscent of the worst of company towns of old.

---

[131] Virginia Commonwealth University (n.d.). *Company Towns: 1880s to 1935*. Social Welfare History Project. Retrieved December 12, 2024, from https://socialwelfare.library.vcu.edu/organizations/labor/company-towns-1890s-to-1935/

Perpetual surveillance with strict curfews, rules, and regulations, and the ability to lock up, lock out or starve a person or family, possibly, to death would make these 15-minute cities worse still. And, once the people's brains are tied to the AI Cloud, those who have survived the nano-technological and graphene infused 'medicinal cures' and 'razors', will find themselves controlled physically, psychologically, mentally, and emotionally.

You must know with profound certainty, that these 15-minute cites will be all-encompassing prison-gulag-concentration camp systems on 24 hour surveillance. Freedom will become one of the lost words along with so many other that, perhaps, spoke to a somewhat better 'experience.' Now, should they have their way, the entirety of your avatar's experience and thus your Infinite Spirit (Chapter Six) will be tied to a concentration-camp 'world', eternally. Further, understand that these are the cities, in many cases, which they are creating by 'fire', by burning them down to the ground. And this is followed by door-to-door campaigns to purchase (see BlackRock), for pennies on the dollar, what remains, in order to build their concentration-camp cites (See LA, Maui, etc.). See the tale-tell signs: 1. empty reservoirs prior to the fires, insurance policy cancellations just prior to the fires, failures to rebuild long after the fires. Questions. What kind of a fire carbonizes bodies, but does not burn them down to the bone or burn the hair or fur (animals) on them? What kind of a governor smiles and dances gleefully as the homes of his constituents burn down?

## THE PLAN 4 - DIMENSIONAL ACCESS/ CONTROL

The final though primary part of the cabals' plan is tighter control over the matrix itself. Further, their ability to enter the matrix, via the in-body, graphene-laced, nanotech transmitters/receivers, brain implants, at will, is another. It is the up-close and personal cultivation of low-vibrational energy that the monsters of the movie *Monsters, Inc* applied. It is what the final goal has always been. I return to the earlier used reference of *Star Trek's* Holodeck. It should, however, be noted that there is a reason for this fear on the part of the cabals', that I will speak to in a later chapter.

The *Star Trek: The Next Generation's* Holodeck serves as the crews' rest and relaxation program. All they need do is to select their adventure, represented by a holographic program, and enter. And when they're done, they just say, "End Program." I then introduced a more sinister version of the Holodeck, wherein their memories were erased and they had forgotten, completely, that they were in a holographic simulation. To them, this place was home and had always been so. And anyone who would say otherwise was 'Crazy'. Thus they had become unaware, completely, of the "End program" protocol or where they truly were.

Now to go a step further, ever-tighter control of those in the Holodeck would be the removal of their free will. They would no longer be able to go/travel where they wished, to eat what they wanted, to live where they wanted, or to have a thought or opinion contrary to the status quo. It would be a 'waking' form of zombification. In the Holodeck this might be done via a holographic brain implant or via a holographic doctor. Thus a simulation within a simulation, a tyranny within a tyranny would exist.

Now, zoom out of science fiction to the 'real world'. The constraints on 'humanity' as proposed by the cabals are to: limit what you eat, limit where and how far you can travel, limit your opinions and beliefs, and limit where you live. There is a concerted effort to introduce a Digital Currency Initiative, as coupled to the AI Cloud, which would track your every purchase, your every 'smart' phone call, your every 'smart' text, your every internet search or visit, comment, your political affiliation, your sexual proclivity, etc. Now via the graphene-laced, biotoxins which have spread in-body, self-replicating, nano-sized transmitter/receivers, your brain implant may well be forming or have already formed. And should anything you do prove contrary to the status quo...

This is the reason for the simulation within a simulation, which provides for that ever-tighter control and, in truth, zombification. It is the book/movie *1984* at a quantum level or two above the book's/movie's premise. And you are in it. The cabals' next moves will determine the timing.

*The Matrix* now is the most apt analogy. Agent Smith and other agents of *The Matrix* were able to access anyone who was hardwired into the matrix. This will soon be apropos and means that anyone with the in-body, self-replicating graphene transmitters/receivers may well be accessible. Though the entity in question would be a much darker entity than Agent Smith.

The purpose of this intervening simulation ties directly to the cabal-above's dimension, where our Infinite Spirits are 'mainframe' connected and 'stored'. The point of it all is to cut off, to separate entirely, to attempt to remove the existing links from our Infinite Spirits to their bio-holographic constructs—human bodies (avatars). The avatars in return will be energy-generating zombies.

Why? Fear. There is little doubt, given the cabal-above's resources, it is their matrix after all, that anomalies were developing across their matrix. These anomalies would be directly proportional to the quickly deteriorating situation within their Earth-matrix construct. The cause would be twofold. The first, would be as a direct result of the cabal-below. It would be the cabal-below's unrelenting greed, its far-flung destruction, its rampant psychopathy, the growing transparency of their lies, the arrogance in fetishing their quite evil rulers (see Satanic Public Rituals: Olympics, Super bowls, etc.). This would be the catalyst for speeding up what was already happening—the awakening of the Infinite Spirits currently entrapped in this simulation. Their abject perfidy has rung the alarm on, "It's time for Infinite Spirits to return Home".

Fear, you see, drives both the cabal-above and the cabal-below, it is the frequency in which they find comfort and take their low-vibrational meals, while they burn the world to reap them.

The balance of the cabals' campaign has, indeed, included the fraud of climate change, another driver in the control paradigm. And in this they are mightily assisted by legions of cult-programmed, 'climate activists' unable to see the clear contradictions in their narratives. The contradictions in pushing for 'climate change', while those atop the scheme get ever richer and war and warmongers get a pass or are actively campaigned for by 'climate activists'. In the scheme of things war would most likely be the number one driver of 'climate change' if, in fact, 'climate change' was even a thing.

This then has always been the core of the plan—to quash the growing awareness of the Infinite Spirits 'contained', for now, in their dimension and within the cabal-above's simulation. They are almost there with the one ring—Digital Currency Initiative—to rule them all. Though 'almost' can be a very long way away and especially so, when Infinite Spirits are awakening and in ever greater numbers.

## EVERYTHING IS IN PLACE

You've been wearing a simulation helmet and the accompanying kit from the time of your 'birth'. Thus you exist in a simulated world called 'Earth'. It is *Star Trek's* Holodeck at scale, though much more sinister. It is the *Matrix*'s Construct, *Ready Player One*'s OASIS, *Dark City*'s perpetually dark city, *Black Mirror*'s "San Junipero" or its "Fifteen Million Merits" or its "Nosedive"[132], *The Truman Show* in its entirety, etc. but in every case it is still more sinister. The 'life' that you believe you are living is, truly, stranger than fiction and not a life at all.

[132] *Black Mirror* (2011-2023), interestingly, has content, which, from its beginning, closely mirrored the times at hand regarding implants, alternate dimensions, social credit, human/avatar energy production, etc.

You are being farmed and the feed is fear and ignorance, war, chaos, and duality—division, fragmentation, race, religion, skin color, country of origin, etc. The produce of which is hatred, anxiety, depression, sadness, anger, etc. This is the food—low-vibrational energy—that the non-human, reptile-like, dimensional entities—the cabal-above seek. Inversion is also a much used feed tool.

This is why there is war all the time, that hatred of the other—race, ethnicity, religion, immigrant, nationality, poor—is stoked and is unceasing. It is why so much is spent on war to the detriment of social/economic/educational uplift. It is why there is inversion across the entire socio-political, educational, legal, financial, and economic landscape. The result: schools do not teach, public/private health concerns do not cure, they kill, the legal profession does not protect those who are most in need, governments ignore both constituencies, their people, etc.

Whether it is arrogance or a must regarding protocols of which we are not now aware, the plans of those in control, the cabals, always appear in plain sight first—predictive programming. They are like unassembled puzzle pieces waiting to be assembled. I pointed out in the chapter "Life on Earth", prior to the acts of destruction, they appear in plain sight, whether through media or a 'rehearsal (Event 201)' of what is to come. And, generally, those who begin to assemble the pieces, to see an uncanny and troubling resemblance to their 'actual' world are ridiculed, censored, banned, or called "conspiracy theorist".

The Plan, as outlined above, was the step-by-step process in which the 'COVID-19' event was shaped, coordinated, practiced, and executed. And whereas a normal medicine/'vaccine' would have long been pulled from the market with but a tiny fraction of comparative adverse events, the 'COVID-19 vaccines' endure 1.5 million adverse events and counting. These adverse events from the 'COVID-19 vaccines', again, were more than the combined adverse events of all vaccines over a 32 year period. And it is critical to understand that the reports which make it to the government's VAERS database are but one percent (1%) of total potential cases. This one percent (1%) is the government's own calculation. As has been written above and repeated here for emphasis, on January 20, 2021, approximately 80%[133] of the US population, which was then 332,048,997[134], received at least one 'COVID-19 vaccine'. The number of the adverse events extrapolated from the government's one percent (1%) is mind boggling.

It is very important to understand that 'COVID-19' was a world-wide, cult-programming event or MKULTRA gone public. The 'COVID-19 vaccines' would, among other things, lead millions to their deaths, maimings, severe disabilities, and eventually to a deeper form of enslavement. It is why those who have been programmed into the 'COVID-19' cult are so impossibly difficult to reach. It will take cult

---

133 Haseman, J. (2021, January 14). *Tracking COVID-19 vaccine distribution by state: How many people have been vaccinated in the US?* Retrieved November 19, 2024, from https://www.usatoday.com/in-depth/graphics/2021/01/14/covid-vaccine-distribution-by-state-how-many-covid-vaccines-have-been-given-in-us-how-many-people/6599531002/

134 Neilsberg (24, August 1). *United States Population by Year*. Retrieved November 19, 2024, from https://www.neilsberg.com/insights/united-states-population-by-year/#:~:text=In%202022%2C%20the%20population%20of,United%20States%20increased%20by%2051%2C125%2C146

deprogramming techniques to free them from this cult of exploitation, death, and slavery.

What has happened via the 'COVID-19 pandemic' will go down as the most vile, democidal, and 'antihuman' atrocity of our collective experience. There is no prior genocide, no prior war that will have come close, as the numbers of the dead continue to mount into the tens of millions worldwide. Only a worldwide nuclear war will supplant this atrocity.

As above so below—there is great disintegration and desperation across the 'country', the 'world' and all aspects thereof. There is the very distinct feeling that as goes the matrix, the simulation, so go those who impose it upon us. The tightening down for ever greater control, the ongoing democide, the human branding via in-body, RFID, graphene nano-chips, the 'Smart Cities', Bio-ID cards, the unending lies to conceal it are all symbols. They are symbols that represent the loss of control and fear—as below so above.

And when failure is imminent, there may well be an even greater reset, one that in an instant wipes 'humanity' from the 'Earth's' face an extinction level event and, apparently there have been several. Why is this so in a holographic simulation, that is producing ever-greater levels of low-vibrational energy? Fear.

One has but to be aware of the paths of extinction level events across the millennia, the disappearance of great and storied civilizations to understand that programs fail, regardless of their advancement and sophistication. And when they do, one imagines Infinite Spirits waking up and ready to return home.

The cabal-above, as I've stated, knows it all and well. And the balance—the cabal-below—know what they need to know and no more. What the cabal-below doesn't appear to know, is that they too are quite expendable. And as things degenerate for this iteration of the bio-holographic matrix, so too will their fates. Is it ever possible to trust a psychopath? No, it is just a matter of time.

This is when Infinite Spirits awaken from their memory-purged sleep, the bio-holographic matrix, the exploitative simulation to the truth of things—who they are. No doubt, a most dreaded outcome by the cabals.

The final truth of this is all around you. You are in a dimensional simulation, a matrix, a waking dream, having an experience, which is, possibly, one of many that you have had. That it does not need the headset or associated kit as we know or envision it, does not make it any less a simulation or an experience of entrapment. It is an experience, however, that seeks to 'recycle' us—Infinite Spirits—forever to its own narrow, exploitative, and psychopathic purpose.

But take heed, there is an awakening of Infinite Spirits from this bio-holographic matrix, across this dimension. This is and has always been a fait accompli, as the finite always ends and Infinite Spirits cannot be kept ignorant of who they are indefinitely. I imagine as things have gotten worse, more Infinite Spirits have continued to awaken. That said, there are important steps to awakening and to leaving this bio-holographic simulation, this matrix.

# CHAPTER FOUR

## Unplugging from the Matrix

> "You have to understand, most of these people are not ready to be unplugged. And many of them are so inured, so hopelessly dependent on the system, that they will fight to protect it."
>
> —Morpheus, *The Matrix*

There it is so very clearly in the above quote and the stakes are supremely high. In the balance lie a complete lack of awareness, eternal slavery, and zombification—simulation within a simulation. On the other side is awareness of one's true self—an Infinite Spirit (Chapter Six)—eternal freedom and Home, Infinite Reality (Chapter Seven).

There is an episode of the *Twilight Zone*'s second season (1996), episode six, which is called the "Deprogrammers". In this episode a reptilian-like, alien race (cabal-above?) has taken over the Earth and have programmed/brainwashed the survivors to be their slaves. Again, the clues of our predicament, via predictive programming, are all around us, we have simply to raise our heads and see them.

A rebel group of free humans kidnaps one of the enslaved humans and deprograms him. There is a twist and it does not end well for the 'deprogrammed' human. I will not disclose the ending for those who may not have seen it. However, to look around at the different machinations, this political party, then that party to replace it, and then to expect different results is, perhaps, an apt parallel.

There are, however, no twists via the writings within this book. This information is provided to free you from the nonstop, cult programming that has attended you from your cradle and, possibly, to your grave. Understand, that in concert with 'schooling', the controlled media, government propaganda there has never been a campaign of cult-programming/ brainwashing more pervasive than there is today.

One answer to the life-long programming is to self-deprogram so as to awaken from the 'Earth' based simulation. Know, however, that the process of self-deprogramming is extremely difficult, and, perhaps, the most difficult thing that you will have ever done. But it is not impossible.

It has been a slow-motion process for me, as my disconnection from media—the news and TV altogether—began nearly 20 years ago. Separation from social media, entirely, began with the onset of 'COVID-19'. I had only ever passively given attention to social media, the exception was LinkedIn. However, when LinkedIn continued to censor the information that I was providing from insiders and whistleblowers, formerly of big pharma and big medicine, I saw the endgame. When LinkedIn asked me to stop, I said that I wouldn't. My LinkedIn account was closed down. And the only 'smart' equipment that I have ever had is my phone. It is very seldom used, rarely checked, always kept at a distance, and never in the bedroom. How much this helps, I do not know, but even our symbolic actions move us forward, help us to awaken.

You, however, do not have the luxury of a slow-motion disconnect or slow-motion self-deprogramming, as the cabals' plans move quickly forward and you are in the crosshairs. Know this.

Far too many have already fallen for the 'COVID-19 pandemic, vaccine' plan and the measures that surround it. Those who are still well ensconced in the cult, will continue to inject 'COVID-19 vaccine and booster' biotoxins and they will continue to suffer the immediate, short-term, longterm results. They will not see this book and they will not read it, because they are not ready to.

One of my younger cousins is dead of turbo cancer. Its onset was immediate, his life thereafter short. He leaves a family of three behind. He would not have read this book as he was not ready to. 'COVID-19 vaccine' mandates, no doubt, took his life.

Even for those who, at first, fell for the 'COVID-19 pandemic' and took the 'COVID-19 vaccines' or 'boosters', and are still alive, it is not too late. There is still time, a way out.

Again, it will be extremely daunting to unplug from the 'Earth'-matrix, control system, the simulation. And it will be impossible for a great many, who will choose to put this book down instead of following through. De-programming was never easy even with the aid of trained de-programmers. Self-deprogramming will be a great deal more difficult, but it can be done.

"Why should I self-deprogram?", you ask. The simple answer is to see where you are. The programming that you have received has resulted in your exploitation, indentured-slavery which pose as 'freedom', then death, and then reincarnation (repeat cycle). In this respect, imagine an *Anti-Ground Hog Day* that imposes exploitation, slavery, death, and then repeats the cycle for you over and over with no end in sight. Would you want to be on that ride?

What you see in the mirror every morning, everyday is not you. It is a 'bad copy' of you, an avatar, selected by another, to represent you. You are a great deal more than this. But this image is what they want you to believe is you. Know that it is not. I go into greater detail in Chapter Six about "Who and What You Are".

There is tragic irony for those of you who are of Millennial age (24-44). You have been most inured to the system. Your programming and indoctrination began in or crossed over, in early childhood or adulthood, the era of 'smartphones', 'smart' tablets, 'smart' in-home 'assistants', 'smart' televisions, etc. They were honed to keep your attention, to addict you via the 'drug' of social media and a host of apps and platforms. Then they spied on you and tracked you and even recorded you relentlessly and they continue to do so even now.

The further tragedy is that you have been a primary target. Your rate of excess deaths, for the past several years, has surpassed even those who are over 65 years of age. This as a result of the 'COVID-19 vaccines' mandated for companies of 100 employees or more, where Millennials proved a significant part of the workforce. Millennials, as a direct result, have been killed/murdered in record numbers. This is what happens when a known biotoxin is given to the unsuspecting as a "safe and effective" 'vaccine'. Their most loyal cadre, with their heads forever bowed to their 'smartphones', their homes peppered with 'smart devices', and their stark addiction to social media are the cabals' primary targets. There can be little doubt about this. In this respect, you more than all others should be deprogramming, unplugging from the matrix, regaining your selves and your 'lives'. And then coming to an understanding of who, what, and where you are. It's not what you think.

There is only one reason that I see for this great betrayal. It is that you, Millennials, represent one of the greatest threats to the Earth-based matrix and thus the cabal-below. This threat is your ability to see and understand, to a greater degree than all others, the technological inner workings and, possibly, how to jam them up. And/or to refuse to comply—work stoppage. This can, indeed, hold back the plan, as you are a primary part of the current workforce.

To all those who have not been so diligently programmed, for whom 'smart' has not played a major or significant role in your lives, this will be easier but still not easy. However, the other steps, listed below, will be difficult for all. That said, it is imperative to deprogram, to discover, to understand, and to awaken to the truth now.

To all those who have not been so diligently programmed, for whom 'smart' has not played a major or significant role in your lives, this will be easier but still not easy. However, the other steps, listed below, will be difficult for all. That said, it is imperative to deprogram, to discover, to understand, and to awaken to the truth now.

## GOVERNMENT, MAINSTREAM MEDIA, ETC.

There is, perhaps, not a single government official who has not lied to you about the 'COVID-19 pandemic' or the 'COVID-19 vaccines'. There is not a single mainstream media TV news station, newspaper, online mainstream media concern, mainstream media radio station, etc. that has not lied to you with regard to the 'COVID-19 pandemic' or the 'COVID-19 vaccines'. The various 'fact checkers', who are paid by elements of the mainstream media or private or government allied agencies do not 'fact check' the mainstream narrative.They do not call its 'facts' into question or ever overturn them. However, they are content to distort the truth to you on nearly every important topic of concern. Debunking scientists, professors, former big pharma executives, doctors, and nurses, who told the truth, truths that are now being validated everyday was the 'fact checkers' most favorite pastime.

The 'COVID-19 vaccines' were never "safe and effective", they were never even 'vaccines', in the classical/historical sense. And the numbers of fatalities, maimings, severe disabilities as a direct result of the 'COVID-19 vaccines' are at democidal levels and rising across the world. Though governments, the media, 'fact checkers' will not see this, despite World War II level casualties. It is a 'mystery' to them, which they deem "Cause Unknown". Where is their "follow the science" to solve this question? It is unavailable for comment. Their "follow the science" is also unavailable to debate those professionals, who have long since seen the truth of things, a truth that can no longer be hidden. The smoking guns of this are many and everywhere. And more such truths continually surface, as actual doctors and scientists and researchers do the real work and do not parrot the mainstream propaganda, the big lie.

What does a rational person do when they discover that they have been consistently lied to by their government, the media, and the 'fact checkers', people that they trusted? Lies which have led to over a million and a half adverse events (only 1% reported), and, no doubt, millions of deaths, millions of severe disabilities. Still, these very same people continue to lie to you in the face of overwhelming evidence to the contrary?

A rational person abandons them, entirely. They pull back from the oceans of misinformation and lies and look for other sources of information. They come to the understanding that they are not children and that they can make their own decisions. So those who attempt to make your decisions for you by censoring information are doing you a great disservice and are, at best, condescending. This in and of itself should be a clue as to who's telling the truth and who is trying to hide it. In the latest episode your government, mainstream media, etc. were the ones guilty of lying and censorship to hide from you not just different perspectives, but the growing evidence, the truth.

Certainly, in the case where there was/is a payoff/ quid pro quo—in funding, advertising, salaries, etc—

everything said should, at least, be questioned, if not discarded outright. Remember conflict of interest?

Pharma's continual, multi-million dollar payoffs to the collective mainstream media via its countless ads is a smoking gun. Those government officials who have received campaign contributions from the various pharmaceutical companies, over the course of their political careers, is another smoking gun. And the hospitals that were paid so much for a 'COVID-19' diagnosis, so much for placing a patient, regardless of need, on a ventilator, so much for classifying a patient's death, regardless of how they actually died, as dying from 'COVID-19' are all smoking guns. The truth of this could not be more evident or more clear. And that there are still people who cannot see this is very troubling (see Cult Programming).

A last point is this. The fact that so many government officials and politicians the world over chose to evade the mandate, to avoid the 'COVID-19 vaccinations, boosters', should be a crystal clear sign, another neon, 50 foot, trumpeting elephant in the room. Remember, they were privy to the contracts with big pharma, they knew what the 'COVID-19 vaccinations' were—biotoxins posing as vaccines. They were aware of the damage and death that the 'COVID-19 vaccines' would cause from the pharma companies own documents (see FDA). Thus the 'COVID-19 vaccines' were not, at all, for them, they were for you, us. So, they mandated the 'COVID-19 vaccines' for you, your children, new born babies, pregnant mothers, everyone else, but them. This brings a new dimension to the lie—prior knowledge of its toxic affects—and yet another smoking gun and, no doubt, a crime against humanity.

As I write, a new president has been voted into office, amidst waves of euphoria or waves of dread. But the only thing that will change is a worsening of the current situation. The pell-mell rush to implement AI and the AI Cloud and all the other programs fetished by the cabals continues, unabated. His cabinet and other appointments confirm this with great certainty. It is the new President, after all, who brought to fruition, through Operation Warp Speed, the 'COVID-19 vaccine'. The ongoing democide of the biotoxin, even now, crisscrosses the land killing firstborns and all the others, who succumbed to the lies of 'COVID-19'. And should there be changes, they will be but the makeup on a long decayed cadaver, the lipstick on a long dead pig. One need simply pay attention to see the truth of this.

The bottom line of this section is this: divorce yourself, entirely, from any and all aspects of government, inclusive of voting, the mainstream 'news' media, regardless of platform, and 'fact checkers', who continue to spread and to 'validate' the lies. It could not be more important to unplug from them. They are not your friends. And to say "No, I will not follow your mandates", is your first step in unplugging from the matrix.

## TELEVISION, COMPUTERS, 'SMART' DEVICES, SOCIAL MEDIA, ETC

On a plane trip home to San Francisco from New York, I sat across from a woman, who had five children.

Over the next several hours she told me about her family and that she and her husband had been done with public school and also television. "It was time for a change and we made that change", she said.

What followed was this woman telling her children, who were all young, elementary to middle-school age, that they were going to be homeschooled. And that, further, there would be no TV in their home. The lack of the TV brought utter dismay to her five children. "This was not well taken, at all," she recalled.

Shortly, thereafter, homeschooling began and things started out very poorly and there was much upset and crying and grumbling. Though with time, several weeks, things slowly began to get better. TV was still a major issue, which resulted in boredom and anger and with the kids, simply, not knowing what to do. There had alway been TV.

She recalled with a smile, "The TV thing took time, several months. But they eventually learned how to explore and how to play and how to play together." She told me how they wrote and told their stories, played boardgames and made up games of their own. "They learned not only how to entertain themselves but their brothers and sisters and us", she remembered. "Boredom," she said, "slowly drifted away".

She noted, with time, that their reading comprehension improved dramatically, along with their vocabularies, their inquisitiveness, and that all other academic abilities had improved or were greatly improving. "It was as if they were different children. They were confident, self assured, and quiet reflection became a part of their lives. It was like a small miracle," she said.

It has been close to twenty years since I spoke with her, but I will never forget our conversation on that plane. It spoke to both an epiphany on her part and, perhaps, a miracle on the part of her children. The children and their parents had, literally, found themselves without the TV in their lives.

Ironically or not, it has been close to 17 years since I've owned a television or had one in my own home. And I have always thought it inappropriate to have one in the bedroom. To date, I write, read, listen to audiobooks, listen to music, watch movies on my computer monitor with my 'old-school' DVD player, and to FM radio, that is free of ads. I'm also thinking of a VHS player. Her influence? No doubt.

In terms of my working life, I have a TV monitor and a Mac Mini with my mini wired directly to the ethernet and Wi-Fi turned off. I do have two other laptops but they are never used, uncharged, and possibly with long dead batteries. It is, after all, about limiting one's exposure. And my audio components are likewise connected directly via ethernet. I am considering a CD player to further reduce my exposure and once again, the 'old-school' way.

In 1948 there was a government operation called Operation Octopus[135]. Operation Octopus according to government files was a surveillance program that turned any television set with tubes into a broadcast transmitter. Agents of Operation Octopus could pick up audio and visual images with their equipment as far as 25 miles away.

---

[135] Constantine, A. (n.d.). *The Depraved Spies and Moguls of the CIA's Operation Mockingbird*. Retrieved November 20, 2024, from https://whatreallyhappened.com/RANCHO/POLITICS/MOCK/mockingbird.php

To imagine that the government or that its intelligence agencies have just stopped this type of surveillance or have not dramatically improved it in the last 78 years would be foolish in the extreme, if not incredibly naive.

It is well known that 'Smart' TVs spy on the people in whose homes they reside and there are countless articles which speak to this fact[136][137][138]. Do you believe that governmental agencies, intelligence agencies, and military agencies are not likewise continuing to spy on you?

So, in addition to bad frequencies, 5G, BlueTooth, which disrupt your sleep, you are being spied on in your own home. Certainly a 'smart' phone, computer, or iPad of some sort is spying on you as well. Unplug and deprogram.

---

136 Watch Out: How to Stop Your Smart TV From Spying on You: https://www.pcmag.com/how-to/how-to-stop-smart-tvs-from-snooping-on-you

137 Your TV is probably tracking you -- here's how to stop it: https://www.cnet.com/tech/home-entertainment/your-tv-is-probably-tracking-you-heres-how-to-stop-it/

138 Smart TVs are spying on everyone: https://www.theregister.com/2024/10/09/smart_tv_spy_on_viewers/

Unplugging from TV will be nearly impossible for most. However, eliminating the TV from your home, entirely, will go a long way to self-deprogramming, so as to not be spied on. Yes, sports, movies, TV shows and TV series, soaps, etc. are very addictive, which in and of itself is a rather potent clue. It is, after all, 'programming' as described by the purveyors themselves and never hidden. And short of this, definitely remove the TV from your bedroom. I have noticed that when I go to bed after having watched a movie on my monitor and Mac mini, my dreams can be very troubled. However, when I listen to music or read or listen to an audiobook before sleep, both my sleep and dreams are much much better. Your mileage may vary, but perhaps this represents testing the water with one's toes.

Ending one's addiction to the 'smartphones' does not mean stopping its usage entirely. Instead it is to use it on an as needed basis, turning it off, when not in use, and keeping one's distance from it. Spend time away from your 'smartphone' and don't take it everywhere you go. Get a lead box, keep it in there every now and again. And bowing perpetually to the 'smartphone' as one walks down the street, works out in a gym, eats dinner with a friend is to be a slave to it, addicted, controlled, a 'smart-phone' zombie. Many a drug addict can easily understand this addiction and its control over them. There is, perhaps, no greater connection to the Earth-based matrix than one's smartphone, a major reason for its many addictive properties. Limit to the greatest degree that you can its use. Or get a 4G phone or even less.

You'll also want to eliminate, entirely, the 'smart assistants' from your home. These 'smart assistants' are absolutely spying on you as well and, I believe that the manufacturers have already acknowledged this. And should they be 5G based, this would compound their problematic nature for you and your family. The sooner you are rid of them, the sooner you will be rid of their disruptive frequencies and their spying. In this alone there will be improvement in your experience and that of your family's and you may all sleep better.

Social media was designed and built to be purposefully addictive and to adversely affect one's mental and psychological well being. To repeat, social media was built as an addictive platform and built in ways that would facilitate repeat, compulsive use. The built-in programming for social media would subsequently lead to depression, anxiety, and increased rates of suicide. Further, the social media algorithms were written to be intentionally malicious and malevolent in order to foster envy, aggression, and even hatred (see low-vibrational energy). Given what can only be described as the intentional, pernicious entrapment by social media, self-deplatforming will be a formidable task, but it may well save your life.There is no disagreement about social media's purposely addictive algorithms and the statistics regarding its ill effects are, truly, staggering.

Deplatforming will move you farther down the road of allowing the red pill to do its work, whilst freeing you from the negative consequences of social media. This begins yet another avenue of self-deprogramming.

Computers. The next most important thing that you can do to limit your exposure to the matrix is to limit your time with computers and their Wi-Fi abilities. Using a computer with Wi-Fi disabled and the computer connected directly via ethernet is a good first step. If your keyboard and mouse are directly wired and not Bluetooth, turning off Bluetooth would be an added plus. Again, it's all about exposure and the less you expose yourself, certainly if you've been vaccinated, the better. Again, older computers may well be the best way to go.

Further, put as much space as possible between you and 'smart meters', microwave, and 5G towers, etc. That the latter have been growing and even grew during lockdowns is very instructive of where the cabals want things to go. It is yet another great big, garish, 50 foot neon elephant, as to the intentions of the cabal. And when 5G/Bluetooth are linked to the in-body, graphene receivers/transmitters (branding) the possibilities are ominous in the extreme. This too speaks volumes to the cabals' intent and to your growing vulnerability.

The difficulty of limiting one's electronic attachments is understandable and had I not gone through it myself, I'd think it impossible. It is not. So many of the people around me have already done this and more are doing so all the time. Unplugging requires that you pull yourself back from, if not end, entirely, the various calculated addictions (TV, 'smart devices', social media, apps, gaming, etc.), the frequency disruptions (5G, microwave, 'smart meters', etc,) and the ongoing cult-programming.

Once you begin to withdraw you will find that the brainwashing will slowly start to abate, along with nervousness, mood swings, fear, depression, suicide ideation, hate, and anger. One's blood pressure may even come down and your sleep improves.

Read books. And when you are with your friends, talk with them, eat dinner with them free of phones. Play boardgames and card games, connect on a different level entirely. Another alternative, is an old DVD or VHS player and DVDs, VHSs of all your favorite shows, great for when the internet-of-all-things crashes and find an old-school monitor. Simplify your life and move away from any and all things 'smart'. Get a record player, used or new. Shop for used records on the weekends, which can be a lot of fun.

## PUBLIC HEALTHCARE

> "It's quite possible, early on, that not everybody involved knew what was happening. But, I'm afraid after a few days, you'd have to be a blockhead to not realize what was going on, that what you (doctors, nurses) were doing to your chargers, your patients was resulting in their deaths. So, I've completely lost any trust in the medical profession, because, virtually, no one has spoken up, four and a half years later"[139].
>
> —Dr. Michael Yeadon

This segment could not be more straightforward than to say, limiting, if not eliminating entirely one's connection to the 'healthcare' system in this country may go a very long way to saving your life.

The government's VAERS (Vaccine Adverse Events Reporting System) database has amassed 1.5 million adverse events from the 'COVID-19 vaccines' (though the number may well be greater as you read this book). The number of these adverse

---

139 [Mi_Bu@gmx.at]. Dr. Michael Yeadon - *THEY HAVE INJECTED YOU WITH A BIO CHEMICAL WEAPON* [Video]. BitChute. https://www.bitchute.com/video/3KsqB31LyPPK

events from the 'COVID-19 vaccines' is an amount greater than all prior 'vaccines' combined, over the 32 year history of VAERS. Any prior 'vaccine' that had accumulated but a tiny fraction of a fraction of this total, would have been immediately pulled from the market. Why have the 'COVID-19 vaccines' not been pulled? There could not be another more obvious smoking gun or greater validation for that said above.

Some of the many adverse events that have long been known to be linked to the 'COVID-19 vaccines' are being validated not only in the big pharma's own documents, they are also being validated in peer reviewed studies. Some of these adverse events are:

- Death
- Strokes
- Turbo Cancer
- Thrombosis
- Encephaly
- Sudden Adult Death Syndrome (SADS)
- Myocarditis
- Pericarditis,
- Menstrual Dysregulation,

- Multiple Sclerosis (MS)
- Guillain Barre
- Bell's Palsy
- Blistering
- Herpetic Conditions
- Hemorrhages
- Anaphylactic Shock
- Sterility
- Erectile Disfunction
- etc. (there are literally pages of associated adverse events)

There is even information now surfacing from a peer reviewed study, that had twice been censored—The Lancet, Elsevier—that looked at the most 'COVID-19 vaccinated' communities in the US to, in truth, validate what had long been known.

> "The mean time from vaccination to death was 14.3 days. Most deaths occurred within a week from last vaccine administration. A total of 240 deaths (73.9%) were independently adjudicated as directly due to or significantly contributed to by COVID-19 vaccination, of which the primary causes of death include sudden cardiac death (35%), pulmonary embolism (12.5%), myocardial infarction (12%), VITT

> (7.9%), myocarditis (7.1%), multi-system inflammatory syndrome (4.6%), and cerebral hemorrhage (3.8%)"[140].

This study concluded that out of 325 autopsy cases and "one organ-restricted autopsy case (heart)" that 73% or 245 of those autopsied had died as a direct result of the 'COVID-19 vaccination' or that the 'COVID-19 vaccination' "significantly contributed to" their death. How can something this toxic have ever been considered "safe and effective", especially when the 'COVID-19 vaccination' studies themselves proved unsuccessful, if such studies were at all done or followed through[141].

The quote above and the information which follows could not have been missed by healthcare professionals. It could not have been misunderstood and thus could never have been 'undiagnosed' as

---

[140] Hulscher, MPH, N. (2024, November 17). *BREAKING NEWS - Twice-Censored Landmark COVID-19 Vaccine Autopsy Study Fully Peer-Reviewed and Published*. Courageous Discourse. Retrieved November 20, 2024, from https://petermcculloughmd.substack.com/p/breaking-news-twice-censored-landmark?utm_source=substack&utm_medium=email

[141] Wolf, N., & Kelly, A. (2024). *The Pfizer Papers: Pfizer's Crimes Against Humanity*. War Room Books.

"Cause Unknown". Certainly, it could never have been missed by those who were injecting their patients with the 'COVID-19 vaccine' biotoxin posing as a 'vaccine'. These were first hand results, empirical observations all with a timeline that tied to their patients' adverse reactions, which ranged from death to severe disability. Where was their "science"?

Understand that the doctors and nurses and other healthcare professionals who spoke up, who would not take the biotoxins posing as the 'COVID-19 vaccines', and who would not inject these poisons into their patients were summarily fired. One can only imagine the number of lives they have spared, including, of course, their own.

Those who remained, who took the 'COVID-19 vaccines', apparently, had no problem injecting babies, children, the young, pregnant mothers, the old, and they continue to do so to this day. These medical 'professionals' are the staff that you will find in the hospitals and the clinics and the pharmacies today. Would you want to receive care from them? They cannot not know what they've been doing, as

Dr. Michael Yeadon states above, "You'd have to be a blockhead to not realize what was going on".

Given the above, these medical 'professionals' are at odds with the Hippocratic Oath to which they have pledged fealty. Yet they violate its principles every time they give a 'COVID-19 vaccination or booster' injection to an unsuspecting patient. In partial, the Hippocratic Oath is summarized below.

- I SOLEMNLY PLEDGE to dedicate my life to the service of humanity;
- THE HEALTH AND WELL-BEING OF MY PATIENT will be my first consideration;
- I WILL RESPECT the autonomy and dignity of my patient;
- I WILL MAINTAIN the utmost respect for human life;
- I WILL NOT PERMIT considerations of age, disease or disability, creed, ethnic origin, gender, nationality, political affiliation, race, sexual orientation, social standing, or any other factor to intervene between my duty and my patient ...

That the reigning form of healthcare—allopathic medicine—had long been the number three leading cause of death—Iatrogenesis—whether by ignorance, hubris, or intention, is, surely, an horrific outcome and an inversion of its purpose.

That the 'COVID-19 pandemic' and the 'COVID-19 vaccines' have been used as curatives, while well known, long proven, and tested curatives have been banned is a smoking gun. This should remove any and all doubts of the violation of the Hippocratic Oath to rather vile ends. Though this becomes a great deal more problematic than just adherence to the Hippocratic Oath, it is foreknowledge that what you inject into the body of your patient is toxic. Toxic with the potential to adversely affect that patient's life or ability to live. Further, the use of midazolam/morphine cocktails, remdisiver, ventilators, etc.—have led directly to mortality and, again, serially violated that Hippocratic Oath. That 'healthcare' professionals, the world over, continue the 'deadly curatives' and the toxic 'COVID-19 vaccines' is the ongoing violation of Hippocratic Oath and of serial atrocities, and of crimes against humanity.

One nurse, Erin Marie Olszewski[142], who was working in New York city at what was referred to as ground zero for 'COVID-19'—Elmhurst Hospital—had no problem exposing what was happening to patients. It is well worth watching the hour long video, to have some idea of the earliest violation of the Hippocratic Oath by 'healthcare professionals'.

That Iatrogenesis was suddenly removed from the list of top leading causes of yearly deaths, could not have been more clear. Though I imagine they believed that 'disappearing' Iatrogenesis and replacing it with "Cause Unknown" deaths would, in fact, hide the truth. That truth being that Iatrogenesis, via the VAERS reports, are directly linkable to hospitals and the 'care' received at these hospitals, across the country. This speaks directly to the growing numbers of Iatrogenic deaths, not fewer. And with the excess deaths spoken to by insurance companies, another smoking gun, directly related to the 'COVID-19 vaccine' rollout, this combination would easily lift Iatrogenesis to the number one

---

[142] [BITCHUTE]. Perspectives on the Pandemic | The (Undercover) Epicenter Nurse | Episode Nine [Video]. BITCHUTE. https://www.bitchute.com/video/MIda2dWyq3av/

leading cause of death. This would have been too glaring an indictment for a 'healthcare system'.

Therefore, it is in your best interest to avoid at all cost, a system, which poses as a healthcare system, but has in the last four years, with very high probability, risen to the number one leading cause of death in the US. What the balance of the world will subsequently report of their 'healthcare agencies' still remains to be seen. I do not believe that it will be good news, and especially for those 'healthcare agencies' that followed the mainstream's 'COVID-19' protocols and vaccine schedules.

In the end, can you trust someone, who has seen, personally, the severe damage, the deaths, that the 'COVID-19 vaccines' have caused and yet who continues to use them on their patients?

I am not a medical practitioner of any kind and have never been. That said, if you must attend a 'healthcare' concern, please be careful. And injectables of any and all kinds should be avoided, as even dental anesthesias[143] have been found tainted.

## ENDING OTHERNESS

Otherness is typically defined as: the quality or state of being other or different[144]. I will use otherness in the writings going forward as the antonym, the antithesis of oneness and unity. There is also no more appropriate place to use the long known phrase that speaks to the above: "United we stand, divided we fall". Know that the cabals would have you embrace otherness to their 'heart's' content and to your eternal downfall.

Otherness is rife across this 'experience', these Earth-based simulations, this matrix. Rife because when put to use as a divide and conquer technique/ mechanism, it can summon up all kinds and types of

---

143 Mihalcea, MD, PhD, A. M. (2024, July 30). *Breaking News: Graphene Confirmed In Dental Anesthetics By University Of Colorado*. Retrieved November 13, 2024, from https://anamihalceamdphd.substack.com/p/breaking-news-graphene-confirmed

144 Merriam-Webster. (n.d.). *Otherness*. In Merriam-Webster.com dictionary. Retrieved November 22, 2024, from https://www.merriam-webster.com/dictionary/otherness

low-vibrational energy—hate, anger, fear, sadness, shame, envy, depression, guilt, etc. All of them born from the otherness of bigotry, prejudice, 'racism', and bias. What could be better for the cabals, than this ever-ready, low-vibrational energy source which we, collectively, grow here in tremendous abundance? There is no country, no society, no state or city, no town, no institution, no religion, etc. that does not suffer from some form of otherness—race, skin color, ethnicity, country of origin, religion, religious sect, political affiliation, etc.

For many, if not most, who have been programmed since the time of their childhood to believe in otherness, shedding one's belief in otherness will be exceedingly difficult. It's as if they have been hardwired over generations to accept this illusion, this diseased fruit of a programmed 'reality'. But it is where the masks, the veils of this illusion must fall, less you be its prisoner trapped on a spinning hamster wheel of slavery, death, and reincarnation. Those around you who are not NPCs (Agent Smiths), not of the long ago captured cabal-below, Vichy[145] 'Earth' (the less than 1%), not the hybridized are Infinite Spirits. Infinite Spirits are your true family regardless of race, skin color, ethnicity, place of birth, etc. as this is simply the form of one's avatar in the Earth simulation. I discuss this in Chapters Six and Seven.

Otherness as employed by religions is the belief that because you are not of my 'faith', my religion, my sect, that you are less than me, wrong, not equal, vile, and thus your life is not important. It is this belief alone, this otherness, that has fed religious/holy wars, brutal inquisitions, genocides, decrees of murder for idolators, apostates and non-believers, ritual killings, from time immemorial, and wars to this very day, to the very moment that you read this passage. Do any of the aforementioned acts or wars have anything to do with a God of Infinite Love, of Infinite Peace, of Infinite Empathy, of Infinite Compassion, of Infinite Wisdom, of Infinite Harmony, of Infinite Awareness? No, they do not.

---

[145] The Government of Vichy France was the collaborationist ruling regime or government in Nazi-occupied France during the Second World War.: https://en.wikipedia.org/wiki/Government_of_Vichy_France

Who then is this 'God' for whom war, murder, capriciousness, genocide, otherness, eternal damnation—eternal torture—etc. are part of the script? All of the examples of religious 'otherness' listed above teem with low-vibrational energy. Who are these Gods? One hopes that the fog is slowly beginning to clear away, that congregants, regardless of religion, might begin to see the truth. Again, how is it possible for a God of Infinite Love, of Infinite Peace, of Infinite Empathy, of Infinite Compassion, of Infinite Wisdom, of Infinite Harmony, of Infinite Awareness to eternally punish/torture someone, anyone for what amounts to a finite 'sin', in a finite 'life'?

The otherness of race is a relatively new term in the scheme of timelines. Its existence traces back to the mid 15th century Europe and the early 17th century in America[146][147]. 'Race' since its inception has been

[146] The Center for Documentary Studies (2017, November 2). *The Invention of Race*. Princeton University. Retrieved November 23, 2024, from https://history.princeton.edu/news-events/news/invention-race

[147] [The Center for Documentary Studies]. (2017, October 22). *The Invention of Race* [Video]. PRX. https://exchange.prx.org/pieces/218457?m=false

employed to divide and conquer the world's 99%, that they should turn on one another for their 'otherness' and not the 1%. This would be the 1%, who had inculcated the distraction, the myth of race, whilst they oppressed, exploited, enslaved, and stole great wealth from the world's 99%.This was, of course, a much desired outcome, which has been purchased over and over again by the 99%. In this respect, the 1% or, more precisely, the 0.01% have been served incredibly well by this tactic—the invention of race—for well over 500 years. The low-vibrational energy here is tremendous, indeed, and a major reason for seeing that race characterization continues.

The greater part of my life, I have lived in places where the color of my skin may well have been a minor factor, but never a major one. And the skin colors of my friends were of a near rainbow mix of the colors some prefer to associate as 'races'.

I have  also lived in places where the content of my character was not a point of consideration. The primary point of consideration was the color of my skin. That would alone dissuade people from talking to me or acknowledging me, in any way, or having a rather poor opinion of me without having ever spoken a word to me or me to them. This is a rather pernicious form of otherness that, in the end, is simply childish. "I won't play with you because your skin is darker than mine. And my mommy says that I can't."

I now live in such a place here in the Midwest. Though it has been as a gift to me, which has allowed me to understand my earlier paranormal experience, to self-isolate, to pray deeply, to ask questions about this false reality, this simulation, and to awaken from it.  It is something that my home state would never have allowed for—self-isolation—as I knew far too many people and there was much too much to do. I have the woman, who I had come here to be with, to thank, greatly, for this opportunity. It did not work out, but it was not supposed to. There are no accidents.

Those for whom otherness has become a driving motivation, a cradle-to-grave indoctrination, passed on by yet others, it is time to come to an understanding of what exactly is going on. It is not what you think it is and it never has been.

Understand to hate to see otherness is to be at the mercy of the cabals, who have you, completely. And while you hate, you will continue to repeat their decomposing drama, their bio-holographic simulation of entrapment, until such time as you realize what is really going on. Or to return for another go in the ever-decomposing drama. The choice is yours.

To move past otherness—the other—you must come to the realization, the awareness, that there is no other. And those with whom you interact, regardless of the many things which seem to 'differentiate' you from them, they—kindred Infinite Spirits—are all a part of you. There is only Oneness of which we are all, everyone one of us, a part—The God of All There Is, is Infinite Oneness, not division.

The consequences of this one realization alone will lead to a profound awakening. It is an awakening that is greatly feared by the cabals. In truth, this awakening is already happening and well underway, as more and more of us—Infinite Spirits—began to see what's happening and who we truly are.

Otherness must end and the realization of Oneness must replace it. It is as simple as that. Of the various steps that I have listed above, this is by far the most important, because to do all of the other steps and not this one, still leaves you firmly inside the matrix. It is a place that you do not want to be.

## EXITING THE DIMENSION AND ITS MATRIX

How does one self-deprogram, exit a cult in which they have been surreptitiously inducted from childhood and for which the programming is ongoing to one's 'death', transition? It is no easy thing to do. Nonetheless, it must be done.

I can feel and sense that the construct—the bio-holographic Earth-matrix—is unstable, disintegrating, coming apart, as all things finite do. And the crazed-rush to upload 'humanity' to the AI Cloud, via the surreptitious, in-body chipping (branding), to impose tighter controls, to limit the few remaining 'freedoms', to limit movement is but a panicked reaction. It is the reaction to our awakening, the spiritual awareness of who we are—Infinite Spirits.

Many feel that this is true and my experience also points in this direction. That said, time to do our part and to unplug, so as to disconnect the cables, figuratively, from this simulation, that wages continual war against our Infinite Spirits through our 'human' avatars.

What I have outlined above, is a pulling away from the cult via a self-deprogramming regime that will begin to untangle you from the matrix. Understand that the Earth-based matrix wants you either dead or as a slave/cattle. The truth of this statement is everywhere around you in the mounting deaths, the lies to conceal them, the 'fact checks' to dismiss the truths, the fetishing of AI. Yet the truth still gets through, as though shoots of grass through concrete.

Time to unplug, even if your life, thereafter, bereft of the technological entrapments—TV, the 'smart' gadgets, the various social media—seems lesser and boring. To unplug is to, literally, free yourself and to stop the mental, physical, psychological, and emotional war waged against you every moment.

Know, it is not impossible and many are unplugging even now. I've done it and, in truth, I miss no aspect of it. My overall health has improved, my stress levels have fallen dramatically, I've no addiction to 'smart' media of any form. And I abstain, completely, from social media, and my sleep has improved.

In writing this book, I have spent more time on the web, reading the media, and reviewing the goings on across the world. It's not been easy to reenter, but I know that it is for a short time only and the intended purpose is to inform and to help my kindred Infinite Spirits.

In the end, it will be what you deem most important. Whether to maintain your connections to the various 'smart' devices, to mainstream media, to TV, and social media. Whether to continue to patronize a 'healthcare' system that may be deemed the number one leading cause of death. Whether it be to wear a mask that does not work for the purpose intended but instead does great damage. Or to continue to take a biotoxin posing as a vaccine, that kills and maims and disables. And whether to continue to partake of otherness.

Your alternative is to awaken in the midst of this dimension's experience and to the freedom that awakening will bring. It is also to see this 'life' for what it truly is—an illusion of reality, a simulation, a bad dream, a hologram. And also to see yourself, not as this 'human' holographic construct, the avatar that stares back at you, but as the Infinite Spirit that you are. Yes, you are an Infinite Spirit and not bounded by this illusion or those who impose it on you.

Further, you are not alone and unplugging will not be at your own hands. You are being guided by kindred Infinite Spirits within the simulation and kindred Infinite Spirits from Home—Infinite Reality. These kindred Infinite Spirits have never forgotten you, have never stopped loving you, they love you infinitely. In time, you will come to understand as you disentangle from the matrix that they are, indeed with you. You will soon come to remember and love them infinitely, too.

Greater still, there is the God of All There Is, of Infinite Oneness, Infinite Love, Infinite Peace, Infinite Empathy, Infinite Compassion, Infinite Wisdom, Infinite Harmony, Infinite Awareness, Infinite Love, who is infinitely and eternally with you, Infinite Spirit that you are. All you need do is ask, pray for help of the God of All There Is and it is done. And so it is.

# CHAPTER FIVE

## Reincarnation: The Hamster Wheel

> "And the dust returns to the earth as it was,
> and the spirit returns to God who gave it."
> —Ecclesiastes 12:7

In writing this book, I have made the link between countless media that spell out the cabals' intention. They are, as mentioned above, predictive programming events, that provide very clear and demonstrative foreshadowing. Event 201[148] was such an event at the John Hopkins Bloomberg School of Public Health, five months before 'COVID-19' struck. Event 201 would bear a rather striking resemblance to the 'COVID-19 pandemic' that followed. This is one of many such 'right before your eyes' taunts, warnings, if you will, to see if you are asleep or awake.

148 John Hopkins Bloomberg School of Public Health, Event 201: https://centerforhealthsecurity.org/our-work/tabletop-exercises/event-201-pandemic-tabletop-exercise

Other forms of predictive programming, as earlier mentioned, are provided through various media—TV, film, and books. You would be surprised at the sheer number of media, which have long spoken to where we are. How could this media have gotten things so spot on, literally, decades, if not a century ago. This speaks quite plainly to the fact that if you have created a simulation, regardless of type, genre, purpose, you, as the creator, will know from start to finish how that simulation plays out. Though there are always glitches in the program or hacks, that tend to cause a reconfiguration or a rearranging or even a breakdown of things, a crash.

Some of the films that could be characterized, specifically, in the realm of reincarnation or seeing the light with a possible malevolent force on the other end are: *Poltergeist*, *Dark City*; *What Dreams May Come*, *Cloud Atlas*, *Defending Your Life*, *Café de Flore*, *etc.*

> "Carol Anne, listen to me. Do not go into the light. Stop where you are. Turn away from it. Don't even look at it."
>
> —Diane Freeling, *Poltergeist*

In the quote above from the *Poltergeist* movie Carol Anne's mother Diane Freeling warns her to stay out of the light, to turn around, to not even look at it. This can also be thought of as a message and a warning to us. This warning coincides with the information from a number of others, who have come to understand what the light and reincarnation actually are—a trap. Suffice to say, that it is not what we have been led to believe by the various religions that support reincarnation or the growing multitude of stories from those who have had Near Death Experiences (NDEs).

The mass of NDEs stories are growing in ever greater numbers. This may be additional testimony to the looming failure of the Earth-based simulation. In this respect, they can be seen as an intensified advertising campaign (we need Infinite Spirits now!) and predictive programming for new recruits to the 'reincarnation' or the recycling process. In a 'world' that has gone so incredibly wrong, who in their right mind or, more precisely, what Infinite Spirit in their right and proper consciousness, would want to come back? Even before discovering who and what they truly are.

When listening to the various NDEs do they not remind you of here, the Earth-based simulation matrix? With their line/cues, their rooms and waiting rooms, their boards of judges, and their elders. Then there are their edicts of "You don't qualify yet, but if you improve your spiritual credit score, we just might be able to let you in next time, though I'm not promising anything". Really? Everything, of course, is designed to send you back to the Earth-based simulation matrix to 'learn lessons', to improve your spiritual credit rating. Though just before they send you back to the Earth-based simulation matrix, the memory of your 'life' is completely eliminated and your spiritual credit rating is set back to zero. Really?

These reincarnation NDE videos and even talks by 'experts' extoll the step-by-step process of cueing for evaluation, sitting in offices or auditoriums for judgement, one's 'next assignment', etc. There are also elders and group forums and classes that provide information and answers to why you must go back to improve "your kharma". How this is not unlike a college or employment office or a government or professional interview, or a con/scam,

I do not know. One is hard pressed to distinguish this 'spirit world' as anything other the than selfsame process on 'Earth' with a bit of bliss thrown in to, well, seal the deal. And once you've been through the 'process', well, you are always (always) found lacking and it's back to earth, where "You must atone" for any wrong that you've done. Huh?

The kicker, again, is that your memory of this wrong, any wrongs that you've done are wiped completely away. You are then free to repeat them ad infinitum. It's a sure fire recipe for the reincarnation hamster wheel over and over and over again. How then does one ever learn? One does not, because one is not supposed to learn or grow or improve one's kharma. One is supposed to repeat the simulation forever. '*Monster, Inc.*', or at least the cabals' version, is depending on you for your negative-vibrational energy—their food.

The term 'Bait and Switch'—the action (generally illegal) of advertising goods which are an apparent bargain, with the intention of substituting inferior or more expensive goods—would seem the appropriate description. The switch in this case is perpetual recycling, recirculation, reprocessing, as reincarnation. This is no less than manipulation and deceit and fraud on a dimensional level.

Are these the action of an all knowing, all encompassing God? No, they are not. Though it's not hard to imagine the thoughts of the beings who oversee this inter-dimensional matrix. Such as the following:

> "We will recycle you forever and drain you like a low-vibrational energetic battery for all of your fear, hatred, depression, sadness, etc. We will, of course, facilitate those emotions via the fear of other, duality, war, lies, purposed lack, destruction, increasing ignorance, the separation from truth, etc. We will do this for as long as we can and when we see you again on the 'spiritual plain', the 'afterlife' we will accuse you of the transgressions, which we, ourselves are directly responsible for. They will be the same that you undertook before and every time before that. You, however, will not remember."

Understand, that what now proceeds via the ongoing 'COVID-19' episode with regard to reincarnation as a recycling event, is about to get far more intense, far more sinister. It is the why of the mass culling of the population, through ongoing wars, that no world leader has a problem with; the injections of 'COVID-19 vaccine' biotoxins posing as vaccines, which now approach World War II casualty numbers, and the why of a possible third World War. It is what the eugenicists, who are in very prominent roles within the ongoing debacle, have long advocated—a vast reduction of the world's population. Know that in their calculations the 'reduction' targets not millions, but billions and this is well underway. I explain more about this in Chapter Six.

Though their talking points speak to the carrying capacity of the 'Earth' the truth behind the great culling is, indeed, far beyond this pretext, this lie. The truth behind this is a very important reason to be motivated or, at the very least, to do your own investigation, your own research into what's actually taking place.

It would appear that the game plan via the rapidly forming simulation within the simulation, as discussed in Chapter Three moves forward at pace. This intervening Earth-based simulation matrix is purposed to cut off the connection, entirely, between your Infinite Spirit, that is 'mainframe' connected and its bio-holographic constructs/avatars—human bodies. This will make it problem free for the farming of your low-vibrational energy, as any pesky awakening of the Infinite Spirits will be quashed. Or so they imagine.

Apparently, as Lauda Leon discusses, the majority of those who you see around you are Non Player Characters (NPCs) programmed to make things look real, to be substantive, and to keep Infinite Spirits attached to the dream, the simulation. She says that they are only "Back fill", thus the reason for the mass culling, as they are no longer needed. All others are human/alien hybrids, and incarnate demons or archons.

The point of it all is to attempt to remove the existing links from our Infinite Spirits to its avatar or human body. This would be similar to permanently attaching your simulation kit—visor, gloves, and microphone—via surgery, super glue and tying your hands behind your back. You would never be able to remove them from your body. And from the point of view of your Infinite Spirit, the possibility of awakening, of coming to terms with who and what you really are would have been removed.

Therefore the 'reset' means stoking evermore fear, hatred, anger, depression, sadness, etc. to an eternally captive audience—you. You would be unable to look away at the terror that you are experiencing, whilst producing low-vibrational energy—food for them. Again, the "Back fill" is no longer needed, because you will be eternally trapped and there will be no need to convince you otherwise.

This alone should serve as motivation to not be recycled back into the ever-devolving Earth-based simulation matrix. Again, it is someplace that you really do not want to be.

And for those who would still believe that coming back is necessary for their 'enlightenment' or to evolve, look around. Do you see a 'world' that is evolving, reaching enlightenment or a 'world' that is devolving, descending into ever greater chaos, reaching ever-lower levels of disenlightenment? Please look around.

The prescriptive is quite simple, don't come back. Don't come back, regardless, of who you see in the 'afterlife'—Jesus, Mahatma Gandhi, Allah, Buddha, Odin, Thor, etc.—as it is a trap, an inter-dimensional hamster wheel. And you are the hamster. Even if one's religion mandates 'reincarnation', it is time to break free from it as it does not serve you. Will that religion stand in for your eternally-entrapped Infinite Spirit? I don't think so. Do you?

Regarding family, they have either wisened up at the time of transition and said:

> "No, I'm not going back there no way, no how. It's crazy back there! I was always afraid and always struggling there and for what?"

So, they have either gone Home, Infinite Reality about the same time that they 'transitioned'. Or they are back on the hamster wheel and you are seeing a hollow image, a fake, a simulated simulation. Don't fall for it. Home is calling. Go Home, please. What is Home? The last chapter speaks to our true Home—Infinite Reality.

The road Home begins with connecting with the God of All There Is, realizing the truth of who you are—an Infinite Spirit—and unplugging from the matrix, the dream. Everything, and I mean everything, around you is an illusion, a hologram, a simulation, even your 'human body' is an avatar.

To end this chapter and to reemphasize, reincarnation is a trap which perpetuates exploitation, slavery, the husbanding or farming of low-vibrational energy from your Infinite Spirit. These entities—the cabal-above—feed on low-vibrational energy to our great detriment and to their great advantage. This then is the reason for the diabolical NDEs marketing campaigns, the biotoxic vaccines, the worldwide culling, the pell mell rush to 'transhumanism', the AI Cloud, and thus the simulation within the simulation. They are all aimed at eternal exploitation and slavery with no further need for the reincarnation/recycling hamster wheel or the 'Back Fill'.

**And finally, attach to nothing in this experience, this false reality, dream, illusion, lest it attempt to draw you back. It is a pernicious illusion after all.**

# CHAPTER SIX

## Who and What We Are

> "When you look in the mirror what do you see? Do you see the real you, or what you have been conditioned to believe is you?"
>
> —David Icke

> "Have you ever had a dream, Neo, that you were so sure was real? What if you were unable to wake from that dream? How would you know the difference between the dream world and the real world?"
>
> —Morpheus, *The Matrix*

We are Infinite Spirits, Divine Children of the God of All There Is and thus we are ageless, timeless, infinite explorers of infinite experiences and infinite discoveries, across our Home—Infinite Reality. We embody Infinite Oneness, Infinite Love, Infinite Peace, Infinite Wisdom, Infinite Harmony, Infinite Awareness, as we are a part of the God of All There Is.

In our state as Infinite Spirits we are like what Nikola Tesla discovered even here in the Earth-based simulation matrix. What he discovered was the ability to draw energy directly from the world around us or 'out of thin air' as could be said, by machines which he had invented. Of course, a stop was put to this as Zero point energy would have, comparatively, cost nothing. This threatened the cabal-below's exploitative financial/economic/energy paradigm.

As Infinite Spirits freed completely of these dense bio-holographic 'bodies', outside of this dense 'dimension', we are conscious, spiritual energy. And in so being Infinite Reality is the Source of our Infinite Spiritual existence, our Infinite Consciousness, our InfiniteSpiritual beingness. In this respect, we are sustained infinitely by Source, as we are Divine Children of the God of All There Is, Infinite Spirits. This in and of itself empowers and connects us to the whole, the entirety of Infinite Reality and all within—Infinite Oneness.

Now imagine this for a moment. Wherever you go in Infinite Reality, you are infinitely 'self-contained'. You don't need money or food or a good credit rating or a bank account or even a home, etc. Your home is the vastness of Infinite Reality and you are in complete and Infinite Harmony. I list what I remember and what I have been inspired to remember of Infinite Reality, Home in the next chapter.

These bodies that we see, that stare back at us in mirrors are avatars and no more. We are not these 'human bodies'. Everything around us is an illusion, a false reality, not real, simulated. And this experience is entirely at odds with what we had believed it to be, what had been presented to us. It was instead a 'bad copy' of the experience that we originally believed was Prime Earth on a higher dimension. Once in it, however, the awareness of our Infinite Spiritual selves was hidden from us and we became entrapped in the bad copy. We began to believe that these avatars, these human bodies, truly, represented us, when they do not. And the bad copy has been forever decomposing to become what it is now. This, I believe, and research increasingly proves, that our story is the Adam and Eve allegory with the talking snake as the non-human, reptile-like being, the cabal-above.

This very same allegory is spoken to, represented across the entirety of this simulation's 'historical record'. It is spoken to across various cultures, religions, creations stories, which span eons, as testament to its truth. They too tell this truth in metaphor or allegory and the non-human, reptilian-like beings have always been there as serpent or dragon or snake or reptilian humanoid. There is no getting around this. And as 'time' has moved on and our Infinite Spirits have been 'reincarnated', recycled, to forget, those memories have become more and more distant. I also ponder the 'prior extinctions', perhaps, as 'great resets' on the part of the cabal-above to extinguish the collective remembering of Infinite Spirits, our awakening. Understand this is the primary purpose of the 'great reset'.

All finite things, those things that are not infinite, like the Infinite Spirits that we are, they always come to an end. And what we witness now across this experience of 'Earth' as a bio-holographic simulation, as a matrix is its inevitable end. And the various machinations—'COVID', in-body branding with MAC Addresses and the culling via the 'COVID vaccines' , AI, 'smart cities', uploaded brains to an AI cloud, digital currency are all smoking guns of this truth.

I have always questioned this 'world' that we live in. As a child, I thought often about escaping from it. I had imagined a garbage can spaceship, decades before the movie—*Explorers* (1985)—would depict that very same thing. It was my five-year-old intention that this garbage can spaceship would take me back home. This world just never seemed right. And the adults were never quite sane or reasonable or kind. And as I grew and matured, these same adults did not seem to ever mature. Today, I can scarce believe the lack of emotional maturity of most adults, though Lauda Leon has provided possible answers as to the why.

When as a young child, I had interacted with spirits, who were not of this dimension, I did not know what to make of them, other than being afraid or unaware of what they were. As I sat in my grandmother's New Orleans shot-gun, styled flat and watched the TV selector knob turn randomly, long before remote control, I did not know that these too were spirits.

Perhaps they were simply looking for something to watch. Nor did I know that the old man at the back of the flat, who told me to, "Be quiet now" was himself a 'ghost', 'spirit' outside of this 'dimension'.

Over the years, as an empath, though uniquely not aware of this, in the very early part of my life, I would have feelings but no idea from where they had come. The feelings would range from good to neutral to bad. I had always tried to tie them to things related to me. They were not always related to me, but it took many years to discover this. Then I understood that these were the feelings that I had with regard to other people and places that were good or, decidedly, bad.

When it came to a person for whom the feelings were negative or bad, I'd simply be wary of them. And when the feeling was most strong, I'd stay far away from the person or leave. Yes, there have been those whose 'endearing' charm kept me around for a short while, despite the bad sense. But I'd eventually go away. And as for places that gave off a foreboding or a dark feeling, I'd stay away from them as well.

What this says to me and there are many stories of such things is that we've not completely forgotten or 'un-remembered' who we are. And as such our awareness and our wisdom as Infinite Spirits does, indeed, peak through here and there. Perhaps as reminders or wake up calls, that it's time to go Home.

I attended a lecture given by a former candidate for the US presidency, whom most would immediately recognize. After the lecture, this person stood welcoming those who would shake his hand or talk with him. I had had a very bad feeling from him, an intense darkness, an evil that I could not understand. I stood a good distance away from him and just watched. This person spotted me and looked back at me as if he had been seen for what he was. The look he gave me was very angry and unwelcoming. I left the Legion of Honor, never getting any closer to him than I needed to.

Years later, I would mention this experience to a friend, Matthew Fox, a former Catholic priest, excommunicated from the Catholic Church for telling truths on them, and an author of 37 books. Matthew had had the exact same experience and feelings, with this very same person. He concurred, that he too felt a darkness, a vileness, when around this person. Years later, I would come to find out that this person had been deeply involved in a conspiracy to execute a well known civil rights leader.

When I experienced a friend bifurcating into a holographic 'entity', the experiences of my youth were now tied to my adulthood. What had, seemingly, initiated this event, was my brief out of body experience, that had allowed me to access her 'mind', to communicate to her, without saying a word. It was shortly thereafter that the entity stared at me with a profound sense of evil, as I was leaving. It was an evil far beyond anything that I had ever experienced, far greater even than the person earlier mentioned, who had been an accomplice to an execution.

The event sent my mind spinning. "What was that?", I quietly asked myself, as I had left my friend's home. I would only go a few feet away from her door, to contemplate the experience. I returned a short while later to see if she had experienced the same thing. She said that she had.

That experience started nearly a decade's long attempt to understand what it was and the why of it. There were signs and sayings and whispered understandings, even from prominent quantum physicists, but I was not in a place to hear them or even consider what they were saying. In truth, I fought what was being revealed. Even when I had the proof of what they were saying—witnessing a transparent, holographic entity—I could not accept it. And there is no forgetting an experience like that.

Then I prayed very directly and very purposefully to understand what this all meant. I needed to understand the 'why', what it meant and its importance, its purpose for me. And a short time thereafter came the first of a series of answers to my questions.

I had known of the man, David Icke, for, at least, two decades or more and had never previously read any of his books. I was aware of his premise of alien beings in control of the world but this did not phase me. And prior to doing any research of my own, I would certainly not dismiss him or his beliefs for saying so. The number of times that I had been deemed a 'conspiracy theorist' on any number of subjects, certainly did not set me up to call another a 'conspiracy theorist'. And those who unabashedly wield 'conspiracy theorist' against others, without an iota of research, completely ignorant of the truth are themselves the poster children for the deeply brainwashed and cult-programmed.

In Chapter one of the first book of David Icke's that I had ever read, *The Dream*[149], he stated very clearly:

> "I'm writing this book to reveal all the major facets of reality and control, to show how the extraordinary human story has come to pass... to uncover the answers to the big questions. Who are we, where are we, what are we doing here, where do we come from".

Here in the first few minutes of the first chapter, of the first book of David Icke's that I had ever read, were the very answers to the questions asked in my prayers. And so began my sojourn and my discoveries, which brought a good deal of

---

[149] Icke, D. (2023). *Dream, The: The Extraordinary Revelation Of Who We Are And Where We Are* (1st ed., p. 350). David Icke Books. https://shop.davidicke.com/us/product/the-dream-by-david-icke-pre-order-now/

information that quickly resonated with me. I came to an even better understanding of my experience. There were, certainly, a number of things in *The Dream* that would take a second or third reading to fully grasp what was being said. But it all made sense regarding the 'why' of it, the 'what', and the 'who' of my experience. In this way, it was as if my paranormal experience was both a starting point and a directional guide for the discoveries and information and truths that I needed. And they came and continued to come quickly and steadily.

I read David's books out of order. *The Trap*[150] was next, followed by *The Reveal*[151], his most recent book. Each subsequent book, would reaffirm things that I had come to understand in the prior book, while providing yet more information and confirmation. From there my various sources of information broadened out and I found even more confirmation. Confirmation that extended across the whole of my

---

150 Icke, D. (2022). *The Trap* (1st ed., p. 350). David Icke Books. https://shop.davidicke.com/us/product/the-trap/

151 Icke, D. (2024). *The Reveal* (1st ed., p. 350). David Icke Books. https://shop.davidicke.com/us/product/the-reveal/

'life's' paranormal experiences and to who, what, and where we are.

*The Matrix* movie, in light of the information that I had gathered and continue to gather, proved to be more prophetic, more revelatory, and a great deal more insightful than simply a fictional movie. That said, *The Matrix* also provided an incomplete view of who we, actually, are and who is running this Earth-based holographic simulation—this matrix. We are not 'human', like those in *The Matrix* were. We are Infinite Spirits. And the machines are not the masters behind the throne, a non-human, reptilian-like species is running this matrix. Further, we are not simply being farmed for the 'raw' energy produced by the 'human body'. We are being farmed for negative emotional energy—low vibrational energy—fear, hatred, depression, sadness, stress, anxiety, etc.—produced by the 'human body'. This low-vibrational energy is farmed and cultivated via events and situations, such as war, genocide, democide, purposed destruction, injustice, abuse, poverty, otherness, etc. Given this, 'life' in the Earth-bio-holographic matrix is a good deal more sinister and perverse than even in *The Matrix* movie.

And here I began, with help, to put the various puzzle pieces together. Few ever have all the pieces, though some have more than others. Those pieces of David Icke and Paul Wallis[152], Dr. Rich Terrile, Max Tegmark, Edward Dowd, James Gates, Nick Bostrom, and a host of others have helped to fashion a picture that continues to find ever greater clarity and resolution and meaning.

The consciousness of our Infinite Spirits are fed a programmed simulation, it is we who then decode and render the Earth-based simulation as the 'world' around us. It is exactly as a simulated game would be for someone wearing the kit. In this respect, there is no 'there there', it is only the construct, the dream, the simulation. Again, we are not 'human'. We are not these finite, bio-holographic simulations, these frail, aging, decaying human bodies. They are but avatars and we are not contained by them. This is a truth that I have personally witnessed.

---

[152] Wallis, P. (2022). *Escaping from Eden: Does Genesis Teach that the Human Race was Created by God or Engineered by ETs?* (1st ed.). Axis Mundi Books. https://www.amazon.com/dp/B0BQT4YWL1?tag=bravesoftwa04-20&linkCode=osi&th=1&psc=1&language=en_US#audibleproductdetails_feature_div

Again, if you play or have ever played computer games or engaged in gaming simulations, fully kitted-out, this gives you a very clear and a very precise picture as to what's going on. Though instead of a human kitted-out, your Infinite Spirit is connected, perhaps, in a vaguely parallel way, as were Neo and the crew of the Nebacanezzer. They were attached, hardwired to the construct. It is, of course, a far more advanced holographic simulation, than anything now available in the 'Earth' matrix and, unfortunately, a reason why so many fall under the belief that it is not real.

What David Icke has related of Lauda Leon is that the vast majority of 'humanity' across this experience are the Non Player Characters (NPCs). They are part and parcel of the Earth-based simulation and they are controlled entirely by the simulation's dictates[153]. They will follow any orders, be the first in line for any experimental drug, 'vaccine', implanted chip, and they will eagerly subject their children to the very same thing. Some may even celebrate the sacrifice of

---

[153] Icke, D. (2024). *The Reveal*, Chapter 11 (1st ed., p. 350). David Icke Books. https://shop.davidicke.com/us/product/the-reveal/

their children to the system. Think about it. Generally, every computer game or simulation that you've ever played has a great deal more NPCs than actual players. And these NPCs will fight, oppose you, not listen to anything that you would ever have to say, and try to bring you down, while obeying the system's every dictate, to the very end. Sound familiar?

It is said that they can be identified by their strict adherence to the dictates of the cabals and oceans of truth, undeniable facts, or court released, self-incriminating, pharma documents will never deter them from their 'beliefs'. In this latest 'COVID-19 pandemic', they may well be the vast majority of those who return for multiple 'COVID-19 vaccine' injections and boosters, despite the growing evidence of their biotoxicity[154] [155]. Evidence which has been gleaned from the very pages of the pharmaceutical companies' own internal documents.

---

[154] Wolf, N., & Kelly, A. (2024). *The Pfizer Papers: Pfizer's Crimes Against Humanity*. War Room Books.

[155] YEADON, M. (2024, November 11). *THE PLANNED DELIBERATE BIO WEAPON INJECTION ATTACK*. Retrieved November 12, 2024, from https://www.bitchute.com/video/DLVuieYhJD3J

These documents show page after page of adverse events and these are the same adverse events cataloged in the government's VAERS database.

Not even the 1.5 million adverse events related to the 'COVID-19 vaccines' in VAERS will deter their loyalty, as it cannot, short of a reprogramming. They will find a way to dismiss or ignore the most glaring truths by citing 'fact checkers', though these very same 'fact checker' are bought and paid for and often extremely unknowledgeable of the field in question.

These NPCs are, generally, bereft of the will or the motivation or the desire to fact check any of the non-conforming information themselves. Further, it is entirely possible that they are those who still wear the masks while alone in cars, or outdoors or even while home alone. Again, they have been programmed to do so. Or perhaps, some of them are Infinite Spirits, who have been terribly frightened by the unending propaganda or who have long ago been processed into the cult via brainwashing and programming. This is why compassion and empathy are very much needed.

David Icke says, "That their astral AI mind programs are directing their thoughts and responses". Further he says, "Only their close-minded perceptions and behavior and frequency nature can tell them apart from conscious or potentially conscious humans. The simulation is running them and that means they will obey authority unquestioningly"[156]. He then goes on to say that they will, as a result of their programming, condemn anything that falls outside of the prescribed narrative. This explanation would go a long way to explaining the behavior of those with whom I have personally dealt. Despite degrees, intelligence, life experience, they dismiss without a second thought, a moment of research anything that goes against the status quo narrative. The growing studies and court documents and the mountains of evidence and the scientific research continually uncovered, be damned. They will not hear, see, or speak it.

When I began to write this book questions came out of nowhere as eventually did there answers. One question that came to mind early was, "Are there

---

[156] Icke, D. (2024). *The Reveal,* Chapter 11 (1st ed., p. 350). David Icke Books. https://shop.davidicke.com/us/product/the-reveal/

really 8 billion people on this planet?". The answer or the realization to that question followed quickly via intuition and a growing clarity. It was soon confirmed by both David Icke and Lauda Leon. No, there are not 8 billion 'people' on this 'planet', that consensus is decidedly wrong. Apparently, the Earth-based simulation matrix has been choked full with a majority of "Back fill" or NPCs in order to make it seem more real than it is to Infinite Spirits. Do you believe that there are 8 billion 'people' on the 'Earth'? Have you ever questioned this?

Not long ago, I began to feel that things were changing. Changing on a spiritual level and that the collective awareness of the entrapped Infinite Spirits and our remembrance, was rising, growing. Growing to a point of seeing or, at least, sensing the illusion, the simulation, the matrix. The Gnostics called the simulation the "bad copy" as they believed it was a trap. A trap that we had been lured into, when we had sought out another experience within Infinite Reality. And this feeling is quite distinct and there are many who feel similarly. We are, collectively, moving to a profound awareness of the truth of who and what and where we are. And this is also very much known to the perpetrators of the simulation.

Know that you—an Infinite Spirit—are so very much more than the cabals would have you believe. You will begin to see the changes—the 'happenstance'—which are direction and guidance and confirmation of this truth. And there will also be an unfolding harmony that brings balance and a growing sense of awareness as you detach from the matrix.

A most important step in unplugging from this matrix and remembering is to gain greater and greater awareness of who you are—an Infinite Spirit, a Divine Child of the God of All There Is. This can be established in prayer, as the more you affirm it, the more you will come to both know and to remember who you actually are and this will change you. I know.

It is most important given the above to know this: There is Divine guidance in this as well and prayers should be focused on seeing truth, through the lies. Further, there are not only kindred Infinite Spirits from this dimension, who are in this experience with you, there are kindred Infinite Spirits from Home, Infinite Reality here to help us, to guide us for our return Home, Infinite Reality.

We are all Divine Children of the God of All There Is and a part of God's Infinite Oneness. This is to say, that all are One. Our true Home is Infinite Reality or what some may refer to as Heaven, which I discuss in the following chapter.

You are an Infinite Spirit. There is no form to an Infinite Spirit. You are conscious spirit and thus formless, ageless, and infinite. You can take form as you so choose for any infinite number of discoveries and experiences and infinite possibilities. You are an Infinite Spirit. Know this.

Know that the God of All There, the God of Infinite Oneness, the God of Infinite Love is infinitely with us.

**Again, attach to nothing in this experience, this false reality, dream, illusion, lest it attempt to draw you back. It is a pernicious illusion after all.**

Prayer of Who We Are

I am an Infinite Spirit,
a Divine Child of the God of All There Is,
the God of Infinite Oneness, Infinite Love,
Infinite Peace, Infinite Compassion,
Infinite Wisdom, Infinite Harmony,
Infinite Awareness, Infinite Love

As an Infinite Spirit
of the God of All There Is
I am Infinite Oneness
I am Infinite Love
I am Infinite Peace
I am Infinite Compassion
I am Infinite Wisdom
I am Infinite Harmony
I am Infinite Awareness
I am Infinite Love

I am awakened from this experience
and its illusions, its false realities,
this simulation, this dream.
And so it is.

# CHAPTER SEVEN

## Home, Infinite Reality

> "Death is nothing else but going home to God, the bond of love will be unbroken for all eternity."
>
> —Mother Teresa

This quote sums things up perfectly. You are going home to the God of All There Is for an eternity, no less. There is no coming back, period.

Our true Home is, indeed, Infinite Reality or what some might call Heaven and it is a state of being as opposed to a physical place. It is where we as Infinite Spirits belong and have belonged for eternity. It is both Home and our playground for discovery and experience and the Infinite Possibilities that our Home, Infinite Reality holds.

Infinite Reality, Home does not contain finite structures like rooms, buildings, mansions, conference rooms, waiting rooms, castles etc. So if you find yourself in one of these finite places, after you've transitioned, then you are in some entities processing or recycling center, an attempt to trick you. Understand, even a thousand room castle is finite. How can a finite place hold an Infinite Spirit such as we? It cannot, unless we want it to. Infinite Reality, Home is infinite. Remember this. And should anyone tell you that you have to go back, regardless of the reason, say "No thanks". And pray for the guidance of God of All There Is' to return Home, Infinite Reality instantaneously.

The following descriptors of Home have come to me, as I have written this book. While I provide my memory of Home, take a moment to picture yourself, Infinite Spirit that you are, Home, Infinite Reality and search your memories. Prayer helps. Home, Infinite Reality is:

Infinite Oneness
Infinite Love
Infinite Peace
Infinite Compassion
Infinite Wisdom
Infinite Harmony
Infinite Awareness
Infinite Love
Infinite Creativity

Infinite Imagination
Infinite Possibility
Infinite Bliss
Infinite Beauty
Infinite Serenity
Infinite Joy
Infinite Happiness
Infinite Discovery and Experience,
where each new discovery and new experience is more wonderful, more beautiful, more joyous, more harmonious, better than the last.
And so it is.

Have you ever loved or been loved by anyone infinitely? I'd use the word Agape Love, its meanings are plentiful, but in the face of Infinite Love it too falls short. Infinite Love is said to encompass All There Is and to inspirit[157]—to infuse spirit or life—into Infinite Reality itself. So it is a love of which we, who have had the remembrance of Home eliminated, can only imagine, at this point. Know that its memory returns even now. However, to get the tiniest inkling of what Infinite Love is, do this. Find a moment or moments in your 'life', where you

---

[157] inspirit. (n.d.) *Collins English Dictionary – Complete and Unabridged, 12th Edition 2014*. (1991, 1994, 1998, 2000, 2003, 2006, 2007, 2009, 2011, 2014). Retrieved November 29 2024 from https://www.thefreedictionary.com/inspirit

experienced a truly incredible and profound instance of being loved and/or loving someone. Now remember just the feeling, but do not attach to the experience, as the experience itself belongs to the false reality. The feeling is but the spark to kindle your memory of Infinite Love, Home, Infinite Reality. Simply let it remind you of Home. This is also the beginning of Infinite Bliss.

Infinite Peace? Imagine for a moment peace here even within the simulation. Peace as the quiet and calm, the ease and the lightness of being free of stress, strain, concerns, worries. Peace would be the quiet knowing free of strife or war or displacement or fear or abuse or hunger. Peace would be the overwhelming contentment and bliss of just being and knowing that nothing and no one comes against you, ever. Infinite Peace is all this and so much more, as to be unimaginable in our current state, though this too changes quickly. Infinite Peace is a vibration that touches all and that lends itself to Infinite Harmony, across the totality of our Infinite Spiritual existence. These then are the words that begin to describe the Infinite Peace of Home, Infinite Reality.

It is an experience, as things go, that you, we will soon remember, feel. Know this to be so.

Infinite Love also embodies Infinite Empathy and Compassion? While there are, indeed, empaths, those who can gain a sense for someone's emotional and/or spiritual state or their aura, in this simulation, this ability has been purposefully limited. Infinite Empathy and Infinite Compassion, however, know no boundaries of distance or depth, no otherness. And through our Infinite Spiritual connectedness—all are one, Oneness—the importance and preciousness of every kindred Infinite Spirit is thus sacrosanct. Infinite Empathy and Infinite Compassion among kindred Infinite Spirits are part of the bonds of Infinite Love, which abide all.

Infinite Bliss, Beauty, and Serenity? There are some landscapes, some scenes, even beautiful singular trees, that I have personally seen, stood before, and admired. And on my drives across the rolling hills of Napa/Sonoma, CA with its many vineyards, long-standing trees, fields of flowers, I would experience a feeling of bliss. More often than not prayers of gratitude followed me along my journeys over these rolling hills. My favorite California beaches, from north to south, have always been beautiful to me, regardless of weather—sun, grayness/overcast, rain. They have always provided a sense of both peace and serenity. Early morning, late afternoons, and just around sunset, I'd be there seated atop the low wall at Ocean Beach, facing the Pacific, taking it all in quietly, reflectively, or in prayer. The above said, all this beauty, bliss, serenity pales greatly in comparison to Home, Infinite Reality, and even to Prime Earth. David Icke says, "We only see 0.005% of visual light", to say that we know not what we see could not be more true. This much is very clear. Imagine then the incredible beauty of Home and ever-greater insight and a palette of colors and shades of colors far greater than anything in the entirety of this matrix. It would be as if an incredibly beautiful, masterfully done painting, Home, Infinite Reality, was then mimeographed or copied by a black and white copier — 'Earth' simulation—and presented as Home.

Now, seek out your memories of Home, Infinite Reality as the Infinite Spirit that you are. Let them come to you with regard to the other aspects of Home—Infinite Creativity, Infinite Imagination,

Infinite Discovery and Infinite Experience, Infinite Bliss, etc. You will remember things, through prayer and a quieting of your thoughts, that are unique for your Infinite Discoveries and Infinite Experiences. Thus you will remember moment by moment Home.

Home, Infinite Reality are described as "dazzling darkness", "a blackness that shines", a "brilliant blackness", which encompasses all the description written above, that I have remembered, and that have been provided for me. As David Icke states and I paraphrase, "be discerning, however, in the afterlife, as these dimensional beings have, no doubt, copied Infinite Reality as well". In this respect, the guidance of the God of All There Is should be prayed for, so as to leave this dimension in its entirety and instantaneously upon transition and thus its Earth-based simulation matrix as well. This so that you may return Home, to be Home in Infinite Reality, Infinite Spirit that you are.

The Gnostic of the Gnostic Gospels say that this simulation is a "bad copy" of Prime Earth. Prime Earth, no doubt, served as one of the Infinite Experiences for Infinite Spirits. We would enter, gain knowledge and experience and new discoveries, and then leave Prime Earth when we saw fit. Part of who and what we are as Infinite Spirits is our infinite search for new discoveries and experiences across Infinite Reality. This so that we may come to know our Infinite Spiritual selves. Instead of Prime Earth, however, we were enticed and trapped in the Earth-based simulation matrix, which was overlain on Prime Earth. But the time of the 'bad copy' is over.

The irony is that the cabals' own actions have catalyze our awakening and our growing awareness. We are awaking and remembering in ever-greater numbers, who we are—Infinite Spirits. And there is nothing that they can do to stop it, not even a thermonuclear war. In truth, that just gets us all Home, Infinite Reality, a good deal more quickly. To know this and to accept it, is to arise from a long sleep, to open one's eyes, to both see and sense the truth. And again, you will begin to understand where you are, who you are—an Infinite Spirit—and where you belong—Home, Infinite Reality. You do not belong in this decaying, exploitative, simulated death experience in this dimension.

This is our spiritual awakening and the realization that we are Infinite Spirits and it is time to go Home, Infinite Reality. This is exactly what is happening. As David Icke states:

> "Prime Earth is in the same 'space' you are sitting or standing in now. It's just on a much higher frequency. As the simulation is dissolved, so Prime Earth will appear like mist clearing in the warmth of the Sun. It may be experienced as a transformation to a wonderful world when it's really the simulation dispersing to reveal what it has been hiding from us"
>
> —David Icke, *The Dream*

Suffice to say, what you truly need to know is that the Earth-based simulation matrix has already failed. And whether you leave this dimension once you have transitioned or when the simulation ends, as David Icke speaks to above "Prime Earth will appear like mist clearing in the warmth of the Sun", it all comes to an end.

Know that even now kindred Infinite Spirits of Home, Infinite Reality help you to awaken from this simulation, this false reality, this illusion. They do this so that you, Infinite Spirit, can return Home,

Infinite Reality. Know, further, that they have never forgotten about us, never abandoned us, and never stopped loving us, infinitely. Know that you are Infinitely Loved by the God of All There Is.

Is there any force, any being, any entity capable of thwarting the God of All There Is, who is of Infinite Oneness, Infinite Love, Infinite Peace, Infinite Harmony, Infinite Wisdom, Infinite Awareness? No. Have they—the cabals—come to this conclusion? Perhaps, it is the reason for their fear and desperation and the insanity now visible everywhere in the Earth-based simulation matrix.

Do they even know now that their plans have been entirely irrelevant, futile, pointless, and bound to fail, to end, when they attempted to oppose the God of All There Is?

There are those who would claim 'Heaven' or Infinite Reality for themselves or their brethren alone based on some dogmatic inclination or acceptance of a given being. They thereby restrict all others not sharing their belief. What God of Infinite Oneness, Infinite Love, Infinite Peace, Infinite Harmony,

Infinite Wisdom, Infinite Awareness restricts those who wish to come Home, Infinite Reality? Again, what God punishes eternally for a finite sin?

Your prayers should be for a return Home, Infinite Reality and for the guidance of God of All There Is to that end. I have written out a prayer to return to Infinite Reality on the following page. Please do feel free to use it, to share it as well.

Remember, you are an Infinite Spirit. There is no form to an Infinite Spirit. You are instead consciousness, awareness, spirit and infinite formless, ageless. You can take form as you so choose for any infinite number of discoveries and experiences and infinite possibilities. What Infinite Spirit needs a condo or a mansion in Infinite Reality, Home, or Heaven?

See Prayer in Appendix to Return Home, Infinite Reality.

# AFTERWORD

> "What you know you can't explain, but you feel it. You've felt it your entire life, that there's something wrong with the world. You don't know what it is, but it's there, like a splinter in your mind, driving you mad."
>
> —Morpheus, *The Matrix*

Imagine a pool of water resting in the center of your palm. It is still, quiet, and at ease. Now imagine slowly closing the fingers of your palm into a tight fist. The intention is to never let this pool of life-giving water leave, ever get away. What happens is that the water finds its way out of your palm, regardless of how tightly you squeeze or how carefully you attempt to staunch its flow. And in the end, it is gone, save for the moisture, perhaps, a thin remembrance of what was. However, when you open your fist to understand what has happened, even this moisture soon evaporates.

What we witness in the various staged events and machinations of control—'COVID-19 pandemic' and the'COVID-19 vaccines as biotoxins'; the surreptitiously implanted graphene-nanobots via vaccine biotoxins (branding); the graphene-laced chemtrails; the unending and escalating wars; the looming, planned financial chaos; the tyrannical campaign of censorship; the pell mell rush to AI; a universe of unending lies—is the closing of the cabals' fingers into a fist. All of these events and machinations speak to the unmitigated fear of the cabal-above and the cabal-below, while, ironically, catalyzing the event that they most fear. An event that is already well underway and that progresses evermore quickly with the tightening of the cabals' collective fists.

It fails as its energy-generating paradigm is both corrupted, flawed, as negative energy corrupts everything negatively. It was always just a matter of time, in this respect, with that time near to its end. Divine intervention and guidance and Infinite Love have seen to this. And the cabal-above and their under lords, the cabal-below, I believe, all have some idea of this very thing.

Yet the compassion and empathy of the God of All There Is even for these beings, who have placed themselves outside and apart from His Infinite Love, remains. This is what has stayed His hand from war or retribution or overthrow or any such thing, as the God of All There Is is Infinite Peace and Infinite Harmony and Infinite Wisdom and Infinite Awareness. Know that even this most evil deception comes to an end. Infinite Harmony and Infinite Peace will spread even in this lower vibrational dimension. Its simulation, its dream, bad copy, false reality, that we have called 'Earth' simply ends.

The failure that I once thought germane only to the simulated 'Earth' construct was the failure of the entire dimensional construct. The cabals have failed and its dictates communicated down to its rank and file to see the simulation to its end cannot be fixed.

The awakening of all Infinite Spirits across the totality of this dimension and this experience was always to be. What the cabal-above and its rulers could not see, due to their detachment from Infinite Wisdom, Infinite Awareness, and the desire to be outside of the God of All There Is's Infinite Love.

This was the ultimate failure. The God of All There Is has always known this, has always known that those outside of Infinite Love, Infinite Wisdom, Infinite Awareness would fail of their own accord. And it was always to be so. Know that the God of Infinite Oneness, Infinite Love, Infinite Peace, Infinite Empathy, Infinite Compassion, Infinite Wisdom, Infinite Harmony, Infinite Awareness, Infinite Love returns us all Home, even now, to Infinite Reality, Infinite Love.

Infinite Spirits who have taken the vaccines or boosters or tests, know that there is no fault, no guilt, no judgement, no shame. None. The God of All There Is is Infinite Love, Infinite Empathy, Infinite Compassion. Know that The God of All There Is loves his Divine Children, his Infinite Spirits infinitely.

Know that you are getting Divine help. That the God of All There Is, of Infinite Love is here and will see us Infinite Spirits through to be Home, Infinite Reality, Infinite Love. Know that our kindred Infinite Spirits from Infinite Reality are here as well, even now guiding and helping us to return Home, Infinite

Reality, Infinite Love. And also to let us know that we are infinitely loved. They are our true family.

You are an Infinite Spirit of Infinite Oneness, Infinite Love, Infinite Peace, Infinite Empathy, Infinite Compassion, Infinite Wisdom, Infinite Harmony, Infinite Awareness, and you are an awakened Infinite Spirit as a part of the God of All There.

If this book resonates with you, then you are an Infinite Spirit awakened, an Infinite Spirit awakening, or an Infinite Spirit awakening in this very moment. I pray that this book will be a catalyst for you. And that the realization of who you are—Infinite Spirit, a Divine Child of the God of All There Is—and that your Home—Infinite Reality, Infinite Love—are remembered.

The Beginning...

# APPENDIX 1 - PRAYER

Gratitude for Home, Infinite Reality

I am infinitely grateful
that our true home is Infinite Reality,
which the God of All There Is contains.
Home, Infinite Reality is

Infinite Oneness
Infinite Love
Infinite Peace
Infinite Compassion
Infinite Wisdom
Infinite Harmony
Infinite Awareness
Infinite Love
Infinite Creativity
Infinite Imagination
Infinite Possibility
Infinite Bliss
Infinite Beauty
Infinite Serenity
Infinite Joy
Infinite Happiness
Infinite Discovery and Experience,
where each new discovery and experience is more
wonderful, more joyous, more harmonious
than the last

## Prayer of Gratitude

My Dear God of All There Is,
encompassing Infinite Reality,
and of Infinite Oneness,
Infinite Love, Infinite Peace,
Infinite Compassion,
Infinite Wisdom, Infinite Harmony,
Infinite Awareness, Infinite Love
I am infinitely grateful for you
my Dear God of All There Is
Infinite Spirit that I am,

I am infinitely grateful
to be awakened from this false reality,
this dream, this simulation
my Dear God of All There Is

Infinite Spirit that I Am
I am infinitely grateful
that you are infinitely with me
that you look out for me infinitely
that you guide me infinitely
and in this very moment
that you guide me,
Infinite Spirit that I am,
Home, to be in Infinite Reality,
and I am infinitely grateful
My Dear God of All There Is.
And so it is

## Prayer to Return Home, Infinite Reality

My Dear God of Infinite Oneness, Infinite Love,
Infinite Peace, Infinite Compassion, Infinite Wisdom,
Infinite Harmony, Infinite Awareness,

I pray your guidance to be Home, Infinite Reality,
Infinite Spirit, that I am, wherein Home, Infinite
Reality as a part of You,
My Dear God of All There Is is

Infinite Oneness
Infinite Love
Infinite Peace
Infinite Compassion
Infinite Wisdom
Infinite Harmony
Infinite Awareness
Infinite Love
Infinite Creativity
Infinite Imagination
Infinite Possibility
Infinite Bliss
Infinite Beauty
Infinite Serenity
Infinite Joy
Infinite Happiness
Infinite Discovery and Experience
with each new discovery, each new experience
more wonderful, more beautiful,
more joyous, more harmonious, better than the
last, And I am infinitely grateful that this is so.
And so it is.

## Prayer of Who We Are

I am an Infinite Spirit,
a Divine Child of the God of All There Is,
the God of Infinite Oneness, Infinite Love,
Infinite Peace, Infinite Compassion,
Infinite Wisdom, Infinite Harmony,
Infinite Awareness, Infinite Love

As a Divine Child
of the God of All There Is
I am Infinite Oneness
I am Infinite Love
I am Infinite Peace
I am Infinite Compassion
I am Infinite Wisdom
I am Infinite Harmony
I am Infinite Awareness
I am Infinite Love

I am awakened from this experience
and its illusions, its false realities,
this simulation, this dream.
And so it is.

# INDEX

My Dear God of All There Is,
of Infinite Oneness, Infinite Love,
Infinite Peace, Infinite Compassion,
Infinite Wisdom,
Infinite Harmony, Infinite Awareness,
of Infinite Love
My Dear God of All There Is
I am Infinitely Grateful for you,
I am Infinitely Grateful to be a part of you,
an Infinite Spirit, a Divine Child of You
My Dear God of All There Is .
And so it is.

# A DERIVATIVE 'LIFE'

YOU ARE NOT WHO OR WHAT

OR WHERE YOU THINK

YOU ARE

Infinity Press